_____,

You are very special! May our God of hope fill you

with all joy and peace as you believe in Him,

so that you may overflow with hope this holiday season

and throughout the New Year by the power of His Holy Spirit.

May you be glad and rejoice in Him!

A CHRISTMAS BLESSING FROM

_____

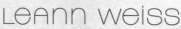

christmas
promises

LeAnn weiss

Regal

From Gospel Light
Ventura, California, U.S.A.

Published by Regal
From Gospel Light
Ventura, California, U.S.A.
www.regalbooks.com
Printed in the U.S.A.

Library of Congress Cataloging-in-Publication Data
Weiss, LeAnn.
  Christmas promises : heavenly gifts for the holiday season / LeAnn Weiss.
      p. cm.
  ISBN 978-0-8307-4697-2 (hard cover)
1. Christmas–Prayers and devotions. 2. God–Promises. I. Title.
  BV45.W385 2009
  242'.335–dc22
  2008048806

Rights for publishing this book outside the U.S.A. or in non-English languages are administered by Gospel Light Worldwide,
an international not-for-profit ministry. For additional information, please visit www.glww.org, email info@glww.org,
or write to Gospel Light Worldwide, 1957 Eastman Avenue, Ventura, CA 93003, U.S.A.

He wants our lives to be one long Christmas Day
of receiving His gift of Himself.
—Charles Trumbull

Enjoy CHRISTmas, it's HIS Birthday;
Enjoy LIFE, it's HIS Way.
—Wally Bronner

*(founder of Bronner's CHRISTmas Wonderland,
the world's largest Christmas store)*

introduction

W H E N   Y O U   W E R E   A   K I D , did you ever make a promise with your fingers crossed behind your back? A hollow "promise" you knew you never intended to keep? And how many times have loved ones, friends, employers or business colleagues made a promise to you that they didn't honor? Haven't we all been crushed or disappointed by broken promises, at one time or another?

What about a parent's well-intentioned promise to be at a child's Christmas play, recital or game only to get stuck in a traffic jam or notified by their boss that they have to work mandatory overtime as they're running out the door?

While writing this book, I decided to do a little unscientific experiment. I purposed to keep my eyes and ears tuned for guarantees or promises. Usually, I skip the commercials on TV, but I paid close attention now. And I intentionally turned off the spam and pop-up blockers on the Internet browser to see what false promises were forwarded my way.

Over a period of several months, I received a barrage of laughable promises. One company guaranteed that I could lose 30 pounds in just a few days while eating as much of ANYTHING I wanted to eat during the holidays, without exercising, liposuction or surgery. Come on, be honest; if I drink gallons of eggnog and eat as much fudge, pie, cookies, cheese balls and other delicious stuff I want during holiday parties, I'm going to turn into the Goodyear Blimp shortly after the New Year, no matter what little pill I'm taking.

Numerous companies generously offered "free" money for my Christmas shopping (at 24 percent interest, reading the fine print), or an advance on my paychecks, which would leave me paying for Christmas for several years. I also received several offers each day for free $500 gift card shopping sprees. (After hours of filling out endless surveys, I didn't receive even one free gift card and was even more barraged by bogus free offers from the companies in the survey for the next few weeks.)

I was so touched when my emails contained several promises that I was personally chosen to inherit large sums of money (seven digits or more) from someone I didn't even know, in Africa. Think of all of the Christmas presents I could buy. All I had to do was send them my bank account number so that they could quickly transfer the funds (I suppose they meant to say "out of" my bank account). You wouldn't believe how many outright scams I received in the guise of help.

Then there were the more subliminal promises of TV commercials, implying that if I bought the advertised present or toy, someone would love me more. Or if I owned a certain vehicle, someone would think I was important. If I used a certain beauty product, I'd look like the size-zero model with perfect skin and flawless hair. If I drank the advertised product, I'd have lots of buddies. Or if I bought the product pitched, I'd be happier or more fulfilled.

I even caught myself unintentionally breaking a few commitments myself, like: "Don't worry, I won't be late" (trying to cram in three Christmas parties on opposite sides of town); or, "I won't forget to ..." (oops, I couldn't remember what I wasn't going to forget to do, just a few hours later). And what about those well-intentioned New Year's resolutions that I failed to keep within a few days or hours.

After I launched my experiment, I was curious to see how contemporary dictionaries actually defined the word "promise," realizing that it's a word that is often abused in our modern culture. I found that *Webster's Online Dictionary* currently defines "promise" as:

1. A verbal commitment by one person to another agreeing to do (or not to do) something in the future.
2. Grounds for feeling hopeful about the future; "there is little or no promise that he will recover."

The verb forms of the word "promise" were even more wishy-washy, including, "Make a prediction about" and "Give grounds for expectations."

Look at the contrast between the modern definition and the definition found in the 1828 *Webster's Dictionary*:

In a general sense, A declaration, written or verbal, made by one person to another **which binds** the person who makes it, either in honor, conscience, or law to do or forbear a certain act specified.

Somewhere over time, the meaning of "promise" has eroded from being a binding pledge (at least bound by honor) to merely a possible expectation or hopeful feeling. No wonder we're cynical when someone says, "I promise." Instead of counting on a sure outcome, we take the wait-and-see, maybe-it-will-happen attitude. And maybe that disillusioned attitude sometimes unconsciously spills over into our spiritual life too.

The Bible is packed with hundreds of promises concerning daily life issues that are closest to our heart. But unlike the world's empty promises, God offers a 100 percent guarantee backing to all of His. Read the bold claim of Psalm 145:13 (emphasis added):

The LORD is faithful to all his promises and loving toward all he has made.

When God says that He's faithful to all of His promises, we can fully trust Him that all means ALL. No exceptions. None. We can take His promises to the bank. His Word is better than gold. Yes, some of God's promises do have conditions attached. But those conditions aren't hidden in fine print; they are clearly spelled out (if you do this, I promise this).

Unfortunately, we sometimes get so caught up in the routine and rush of life that we forget to seek the illumination of the Bible. It's my prayer that *Christmas Promises: Heavenly Gifts for the Holiday Season* will help you personalize the timeless promises of God's Word to your everyday life. May you experience the refreshment of God's one-on-one love as you read the personalized Scriptures that bring God's Word alive in your daily circumstances. May your heart be inspired by true stories of God's faithfulness to fulfill His promises. May God's promises of His presence, His peace, His provision, His rest, and many others encourage you this holiday season. May you be blessed by the gift of His promises today and always, and may You trust in Him wholeheartedly to fulfill His promises to you.

Hugs,

LeAnn Weiss

Encouragement Company

My *stressed* Child,

Let Me enlighten the eyes

of your heart so that you will experience

the hope I've called you to and the riches of

My glorious *inheritance*. I'll show you the

wonder of My great love.

Let Me *restore* the joy of your salvation

and grant you a *willing spirit*.

Lifting Your Weary *Heart,*

YOUR ROCK *of* AGES

(Ephesians 1:18; Psalm 17:7; Psalm 51:12)

childlike
wonder

BELINDA ELLIOT REALIZED that for the last few years she had been
caught up in the Christmas rat race. She raced through malls at breakneck
speed, searching for the perfect gifts. She found herself still shopping at
closing time on Christmas Eve. She confessed that she'd been guilty of
buying presents on the way out of town to visit family members, and even
had to wrap them in the car as her husband sped down the interstate trying not to be late again.

Somehow Christmas had turned into one big exhausting race to the
finish line. Belinda felt like she was always rushing but never able to catch
up. Christmas hadn't always been a blurry rush. She flashed back to
Christmases of her childhood when her neighborhood turned into a sea
of Christmas lights and decorations, and her parents would drive them
around to see all the magical lights.

She remembered the tranquil setting of their home
decorated with green garlands and holly berries,
twinkling lights, stockings hung on the mantle
and a tall tree adorned with beautiful ornaments.
In the days leading up to Christmas, Belinda
recalled how much she had enjoyed lying
in front of their fireplace at night and

gazing at their living room lit up only by the small colorful lights on their Christmas tree.

There was a time when Christmas was her favorite time of the year and a delightful holiday she could savor for weeks.

Why does Christmas seem to lose that magical quality as we get older? Belinda wondered.

Perhaps it was because, as adults, we are now responsible for all the things we never had to worry about as kids—brainstorming the perfect gift for each of our loved ones, fighting the traffic and crowded malls to spend hours shopping, writing Christmas cards until our hands cramp, decorating the house, cooking for numerous Christmas parties or family gatherings—the list could go on and on.

Belinda decided not to let the Christmas rat race triumph this year.

She decided to change her approach to Christmas. She wouldn't let Christmas preparations and shopping get the best of her. Instead, she would truly enjoy the holiday and take time to remember the reason for the season. *But how?*

She still needed to get everything done just like every year, but she didn't want to get caught up in the commercialism or stress as she usually did. She wanted to recapture that amazement and wonder that she had felt during the holidays as a child. So she began with a simple prayer.

Lord, help me keep You at the center of all I do for Christmas this year.

A few days later, Belinda was reading in the book of Ephesians and stopped to ponder a verse. She was intrigued by Paul's prayer for the church at Ephesus: "I pray also that the eyes of your heart may be enlightened in order that you may know the hope to which he has called you, the riches of his glorious inheritance in the saints" (Ephesians 1:18).

That's it! Belinda thought. She wanted her eyes opened again to the hope and glorious inheritance Christ Jesus offers. That's where the true magic of Christmas lies.

Belinda remembered that we celebrate Christmas because the baby born in a stable so many years ago brought us hope and salvation; we give gifts to those we love because we remember the greatest gift ever given— God's Son—so that we could have a relationship with the Father through Christ, who forgives our sins. And as the Father's adopted sons and daughters, we have heaven to look forward to, where Jesus is preparing a place for us.

These are truths that we all know as Christians, but they can often get lost in the Christmas rush when we get "holidazed." Belinda decided not to let these truths fall to the sidelines this year.

As she kept God's promises at the forefront of her mind, an interesting thing happened. The season became magical once again. Christmas lights seemed brighter, people seemed merrier and she found Christmas full of good cheer once again.

Even more amazing, Belinda discovered that as she focused on Christ, the aggravating preparation details that usually made her feel stressed out fell nicely into place. Her house was even more decorated than it had been in years past. She actually finished her Christmas shopping and even wrapped most of the presents without waiting until the last minute.

The best part for Belinda was rediscovering her Christmas joy. Rather than approaching the holiday with dread because of everything she needed to do, she found herself approaching the festivities with the wide-eyed wonder of a child once again.

December 25 was a truly special day with her family and friends, reflecting on the marvelous love and grace Christ has given us.

Are you trapped in the midst of the Christmas rat race?

If so, take Belinda's challenge. Slow down and let Christ take back Christmas in your life. May you once again enjoy this wondrous season with the joy and faith of a child.

My *Disillusioned* One,

Come to Me like a little child.

Put your hope in My good name.

Call unto Me and I will *answer* you.

I'll reveal great and *mighty* things

to you that you don't already know.

My *precepts* are right,

bringing joy to your heart.

And My *commands* are radiant,

restoring the *sparkle* in your eyes.

Let My joy be your *strength*.

Joyfully,

YOUR GOD *of* WONDER

(Mark 10:15; Psalm 52:9; Jeremiah 33:3; Psalm 19:8-9; Nehemiah 8:10)

Following Jesus cannot be done at a sprint. If we want to follow someone, we can't go faster than the one who is leading.

—JOHN ORTBERG

DEAREST FATHER:

Thank You for sending Jesus to enable me to experience abundant life. Help me stand in awe of Your deeds. You're incomparable! Your Name is above all other names. Forgive me for the times when I let other people or things in my life slip into first place. Help me prioritize my relationship with You this Christmas and throughout the year. Father, give me Your perspective on my life. I need You to enlighten my eyes so that I can live in Your hope each day. I'm asking You to restore the wonder of Christmas. Help me enjoy life again. Give me a new sense of appreciation and a childlike faith that pleases You! Let me know the hope to which You've called me and the riches of Your glorious inheritance. You're truly the Best! 🎁

My *Wandering* Child,

My eyes search the whole earth,

looking for people whose hearts

are tuned to Me so that I can show

My great power in helping them.

I AM your *Refuge* and your *Strength*.

I am your very present help in trouble.

No matter what, you don't have to fear.

Never *forget* that you can do all things

because I'm your *Power Source*.

Directing You,

YOUR GOOD SHEPHERD

(2 Chronicles 16:9; Psalm 46:1-3; Philippians 4:13)

18

searching for christmas

WHEN 15-YEAR-OLD Lexi Dominguez ate eggs for breakfast that December Sunday morning, she had no idea how long that one meal would have to last. In a rush not to be late for the 10:45 A.M. service at church, her dad and brothers skipped breakfast, something they would later deeply regret.

Lexi's parents had divorced about a decade earlier. But her father, Freddy, had moved to the town of Paradise, California, earlier in the year to be closer to her, Josh (12), and Chris (18). He now worked as the assistant youth director at their church where their mom, Lisa, and her fiancé, Brian, also attended. Although Lisa Sams was engaged to be married, she and her former husband, Freddy, had learned to work cooperatively with the kids and were friends again. Both families routinely attended church together each week.

Lexi and Christopher permanently lived with Freddy, while Josh stayed with his mom. However, Freddy and Lisa were very cooperative about letting their children freely visit each other. At church, the Dominguez children greeted their mom with extra hugs, knowing that she had just flown home from her mother's funeral. Hugging Lexi for the first time since burying her mom, Lisa whispered, "Lexi, I love you so much. I couldn't imagine not having you and your brothers in my life."

Still fresh with grief, Lisa was anxious to get home after church. She handed Freddy the forest permit to take their kids on a search for the perfect Christmas tree.

Freddy usually fixed a late brunch for his kids after church, but today, they decided to head straight for Lassen National Forest. After a scenic drive 100 miles north of Sacramento, California, Freddy parked his truck alongside the road. The mountain air was a bit colder than they expected, so Lexi grabbed her jacket. The rest were wearing sweatshirts. Her little brother, Josh, felt chilly, so they looked through the pickup truck and saw that their mom had left one of her light jackets behind, which Josh decided to wear.

Before they walked into the forest, they decided they wouldn't pick the tree until everyone agreed on the same tree. When someone spotted a candidate tree, the rest of the family would come over to inspect it. As they wandered from tree to tree, Freddy kept a point of reference to their truck so that it would be easy to find again. After an enjoyable search, they finally agreed on the ideal six-foot tree and chopped it down.

Chris helped his dad carry the tree as they started back to their truck. As Freddy led, Chris said, "Dad, are you sure we came this way?"

"I think so, son. I was watching closely."

After hiking for a while, carrying a tree that seemed to be getting heavier, Freddy wondered if his son was right; maybe they were going the wrong direction. Eventually, they found a road they didn't recognize, and neither did they find their yellow pickup truck.

They tried to backtrack, but the forest became a maze, and they lost all sense of direction. After an hour of lugging the tree through the thorny brush, they finally voted to abandon it. Lexi was getting tired of walking and wanted to rest. Looking at his watch, Freddy knew that nightfall was coming soon and he virtually carried his daughter to go faster, realizing that none of them had a flashlight. When Lexi couldn't walk another step, they were forced to rest. In addition to the coming darkness, it started to snow, covering any remaining traces of their footprints. And no one was dressed for freezing weather.

Lexi started yelling, "Help! Help!"

"Honey," Freddy said, "yelling 'help' sounds a bit desperate. Let's yell 'Hello' instead."

But no one responded to their "hellos," and their cell phones were useless without a signal.

Realizing they had no choice but to spend the night in the forest, Freddy searched for a natural shelter while his children rested. With no caves or bridges in sight, he settled for building a makeshift shelter out of branches on a hill. After Freddy almost stumbled down a cliff trying to haul more branches, he decided what he had already built would have to make do. Unfortunately, the shelter wasn't quite big enough for everyone. Both Freddy and Chris were partially exposed on each side, with Lexi and Josh sandwiched between them. The four of them huddled together trying to use their body heat to keep warm.

It was a miserable night marked by anxious moments. Freddy kept reminding everyone to slow down their breathing and breathe into their shirts to avoid hyperventilation. Clumps of snow kept randomly dropping on Freddy and Chris from the branches above. They could hear the whistling of the wind. Freddy asked God to please stop the wind, and that seemed to help, but it was still bitterly cold. With their empty stomachs growling, Freddy wished that he had taken the time to stop for lunch on the way to the forest. Lexi felt guilty because she had eaten those eggs. With the kids wearing light Vans tennis shoes, their feet were cold. In the middle of the night Freddy felt better after he took his wet socks off. Tomorrow they would get to go home and life would return to normal. As they chatted about current events and life, Lexi asked, "Dad, what happens if no one notices we haven't come home yet?"

Freddy had already considered that possibility but didn't want to frighten his children. He knew that Lisa might not start looking for them until Monday night when she went to pick up Josh from school. But there was a possibility that his nephew who was living with them would call when they didn't come home.

Lexi was right. Actually no one would be searching for them yet.

When they woke up in the morning after catching a few minutes of sleep at a time throughout the night, they marveled at the awe of God's beauty in the snow. Everything appeared silver, sparkling in the morning sunlight. Freddy warned the kids not to eat the cold snow but to melt it first in their mouths by exhaling. Hoping that a search party was looking for them by now, they decided to explore. "Kids, step in my footprints," Freddy instructed, in an attempt to keep them from soaking their thin shoes.

As they walked through the pristine snow, Lexi led them in some of the praise songs she sang as a member of the church youth group's worship team. After another hour of hiking, Chris and Lexi needed to rest, still exhausted from the almost sleepless night. Freddy and Josh walked for another mile. Eventually they found hollow logs that they later rested in until Josh thought he felt something slither over his leg. Josh screamed "Snake! Snake!" which caused them to move quickly until they realized it was just a branch.

Back in Paradise, their mom called Josh's school during her lunch break to see if she could pick up the cookie dough from their school fundraiser after school. When Lisa learned that Josh hadn't shown up for school, she wasn't worried at first. *Maybe Josh didn't feel well, and Freddy let him sleep in.* But later in the day, when she found out that Freddy didn't show up at his regular pest control job, Lisa feared that something was wrong. Freddy rarely missed work and was highly responsible. She knew he would have called in if he were sick. She drove by her former husband's house and learned from Freddy's nephew that they hadn't come home Sunday night.

* * *

Lisa called around and discovered that no one had heard from them since church the day before. Shortly after 6 P.M., she called the police to report that her former husband and their three children were missing in the forest.

* * *

Meanwhile, Freddy and the kids struck out again, trying to find the truck. By mid-afternoon, Freddy prayed that God would help him locate a cave or something that would give them more shelter if they had to spend another cold night in the forest. By this time, they had abandoned yelling "Hello" and were screaming "HELP!"

At 4:00 P.M., Lexi discovered a culvert. Freddy inspected it and decided it would be the best place to shelter. There were lots of rocks, and it had running water that would keep them hydrated. The others agreed that the culvert would be better than the uncomfortable and frigid shelter they had shivered in the previous night.

* * *

Monday evening, as rescue efforts were initially launched, the search was limited to three small search parties joined by friends. They found the yellow Chevy truck registered to Freddy Dominguez abandoned by the side of the road. Unfortunately, the tracks were already covered by eight inches of fresh snow that blanketed the forest ground. Around 4:00 A.M., the searchers called it a night, deciding to resume the search at daylight. Back in the culvert, it started to rain, and Freddy and the kids found themselves lying partially in water. Freddy took off his long-sleeved shirt and ripped it to make wraps for his kids' feet. It was another long and mostly sleepless night.

Regardless, they huddled together, praying and believing that God would help them.

* * *

Extremely worried for her children who had been out in the freezing cold for more than a full day, Lisa tried to generate more interest in the search by leaving messages at media outlets throughout the area. At 6:00 A.M., Tuesday morning, Lisa finally reached the Sacramento media. Their coverage sparked a state and then a national media frenzy. Tuesday morning, the search intensified. Low visibility still confined the rescue effort to the ground. I first learned about the missing Dominguez family when I saw the search nationally covered on FOX news.

Tuesday, Freddy noticed that his daughter's feet were starting to turn black. Fearing frostbite, he had the kids put their feet in each other's shirts and rub them to keep warm.

Rescue crews from the Bay Area and Nevada had now joined in the search. The search party grew to more than 400 people. Rescuers feared the worst, knowing that with each hour the likelihood of the family surviving the frigid cold temperatures without any food were rapidly diminished.

"God, I don't know what to do," Freddy prayed. "Please help me get my kids out of here alive."

They broke branches and used the twigs to spell HELP in the snow. They talked about food, God and life. Josh was afraid they would never see their mom again. "Dad, are we going to make it out?" he asked.

"Josh, if I didn't believe that God was going to help us, wouldn't I tell you what your Christmas present was?" Freddy assured his youngest son.

On day four of their unplanned adventure, Freddy and the kids brushed off the fresh snow that had blanketed their SOS made of twigs. Freddy also added some of his clothes to the area, hoping that someone would spot them.

Although Freddy never doubted that God would save them, he was still very concerned about frostbite and their need for nutrition. He walked away from the culvert to earnestly pray. As Freddy talked to God, he was greatly encouraged when he heard the voices of his children singing "Our God Is an Awesome God." That was a tender moment Freddy will never forget. How that sweet praise lifted his heart as he heard his children proclaiming their trust in God in their moment of greatest need. His biggest desire had always been that his children would love and serve God.

Wednesday afternoon . . . *Finally*, with a temporary break in visibility, the rescuers launched an air search. Lisa knew they had to find her children and Freddy before dark. She was desperately caught up in the whirlwind of waiting without knowing. For once, she was helpless and had to rely totally on God. She kept thinking, *Have faith*. It comforted her heart to know that wherever they were, they were praising God and trusting in Him and believing in Him. She knew that her ex-husband would make any sacrifice for their children.

There wasn't a big window of time because another snowstorm was rapidly approaching. But knowing that the lost family might not survive another night in the freezing cold, the CHP helicopter decided to make one last run to search.

"Dad, doesn't that sound like a helicopter?" Josh yelled. They thought they had heard sirens and other sounds over the past few days, but no help had arrived, and they wondered if they were just imagining the sounds.

Freddy was faint from no food for four days and exhausted from virtually no sleep. But that noise was all he needed to compel him to run out of their culvert. Barefoot, he ran over the jagged rocks and into the little stream before falling down into the two feet of snow that blanketed the forest. He got up and started waving, desperately trying to get the attention of the helicopter. Soon Lexi joined her dad.

His hopes waned as the helicopter turned away. Freddy feared that they didn't see him. But then it circled and came back about 40 seconds later. The helicopter pilot, Steve Ward, thought he had spotted a man waving for help in the snow. Then, helicopter flight officer David White, of the California Highway Patrol, spotted the message spelled by branches and the clothing. That's when they were pretty sure they had found their missing family. By this time, the entire family was out in the snow frantically waving. With visibility rapidly dropping, the pilot considered it a miracle they had found the lost family in time.

The helicopter blades were still spinning when they landed, and the pilot motioned for them to back up. Lexi cried as she hugged her rescuers. The pilot could only carry two of them at a time. Loading Josh and Lexi into the helicopter, he gave Freddy and Chris camping rations and blankets and told them he'd return in 40 minutes *if* visibility allowed.

Eventually, all four were airlifted to Feather River Hospital. It wasn't until they arrived at the hospital that exhaustion finally hit them. Hospital food doesn't have a reputation for tasting great, but the roast beef and mashed potatoes had never tasted so good.

Lisa was at home with her youngest daughter, and sick with a bronchial condition, when she received the joyous call that her children and Freddy had been rescued. She rushed to the hospital where they were being treated. After a tearful reunion with her children, Lisa said, "Freddy, I can't thank you enough for saving our children. God knew that I couldn't handle losing them after just losing my mom. Thanks for not giving up on God or letting our kids become discouraged by negativity." Lisa had no doubt that their faith had saved them.

At a nationally televised press conference, Freddy pointed all the glory back to God. That's when I knew I wanted to contact him to retell his story of God's faithfulness. The doctors were shocked that their condition was so remarkable, considering the life-threatening experience they had survived. People who have been in the cold for just two hours can experience hypothermia. Amazingly, other than Lexi's frostbite and their fatigue and hunger, they didn't suffer any other major side effects despite being in freezing weather for four days. They were all released later that evening, although Lexi was later readmitted to treat her frostbite.

While they were lost, their church had hung a banner that read, "We're praying for you, Freddy." That next Sunday, just two days before Christmas, their church welcomed them back with a special praise service. They prayed over the Dominguez family and thanked God for protecting them and bringing them home for Christmas.

It was by far the best Christmas ever for their families. This Christmas was much more than just a time of exchanging gifts. It was Freddy's first Christmas with his kids in four years and only his second Christmas with them in eight years. Both families spent their first Christmas together since the divorce. Freddy's dad even joined the festivities to celebrate God's rescue and that they were all safe and together again.

Through it all, Lisa learned to rely totally on God. It was something she couldn't fix on her own. Lexi shared with me that being lost in the woods reminded her of the importance of family and working together. She doubts if they would have survived if there were only two of them lost. But with four of them, they used their body heat and encouraged each other. Most important, the crisis drew her closer to God. During the times when she wondered if they would survive, her dad encouraged her with the truth of Philippians 4:13: "I can do everything through Christ who gives me strength," and other promises from the Bible. There's no doubt in Freddy's mind that family matters and that his God is an awesome God who truly saves and rescues His children when they call out to Him.

My *Seeking* Child,

I don't play hide 'n' seek. I listen to you when you call upon Me. When you *eagerly seek* Me, you will find Me! Even when it *seems* like I've forgotten about you, you're never off My radar screen. I'm always *aware* of you and I intimately know you. You're never out of the reach of My Spirit. No matter *where* you are, you have the gift of My presence! My hand will guide you! When you need wisdom, just ask Me and I'll *generously give* it to you without judging you.

Making a Way Where There Seems to Be No Way,

YOUR SOVEREIGN LORD

(Jeremiah 29:12-13; Psalm 139:7-10; James 1:5)

«28»

Life's greatest tragedy is to lose God and not to miss him.
– F. W. NORWOOD

DEAREST CREATOR:

It's so easy to get lost in the distractions of my often-hectic schedule. Sometimes it feels like I'm being pulled by so many responsibilities and in so many directions that I end up confused and tired. Forgive me for the times when I try to do life on my own. When I get cocky or too busy, I get off Your perfect path. Then I lose perspective of the things that really matter and will count eternally. Remind me that when I do life without Your leading, I'm always going to end up lost and hungry. I'll never be satisfied unless I'm following You. Lord, please give me a burning passion for the things that You want me to pursue. Clearly show me Your will and purpose. I want my life to count; and it will if I do the things You created me to do. Remind me that anything else is worthless. Please keep my eyes fixed on You. Be the center of my life. I desperately need You and would be lost without You!

My *Gifted* Child,

You are My workmanship,
created in Christ Jesus
to do *good works,* which I've already
prepared in advance for you to do.

I'm able to make all grace abound to you.

Watch Me *supply* you with
everything you need to
thrive in *service* to others.

Uniquely Equipping You,

YOUR CREATOR

(Ephesians 2:10; 2 Corinthians 9:8)

A Home For christmas

"HONEY, I JUST GOT A CALL from Bruce Prevost about a special project. They need a volunteer interior decorator for a rush project, and I think you're the perfect person for the job."

My friend Coni Rhudy was at a Christmas luncheon with her Bible study group when her husband, Doug, called her about the decorating project. He explained that they had 44 days to complete a redecorating job on a large home.

"But I have so much to do to prepare for Christmas," Coni replied, "and I don't really feel qualified to do a project of that magnitude in such a short time frame."

"Coni," Doug said, "I know you can do this. You've done a great job decorating our homes. Could you please stop by just to talk to Bruce after your luncheon?"

Coni did talk with Bruce. And when he explained that the project was a new home for the Szuka family, whom Coni knew, and that a very generous donor, who was moved by the Szukas' generosity to others, had provided the house, Coni was in.

Doug and Coni had been friends of the Szuka family for more than 43 years. Alicia Szuka headed their church's special needs ministry. Her husband, Juan, had extensive back injuries, and they had two special-needs daughters—Cynthia, their oldest daughter, who has cerebral palsy and is wheelchair bound, and Elisabeth, who has Asperger's syndrome. Their home had mold and mildew problems, as well as roof damage from the prior year's hurricanes.

At first, the anonymous donor planned to have the Szukas' current house repaired. But when he learned that their house wasn't handicapped accessible, he personally worked with a real estate agent to find a handicapped-accessible house and get it totally remodeled in time for Christmas. Many individuals who were aware of the project said it couldn't be done in such a short amount of time. Then Bruce thought of Coni and asked her to be the interior designer.

The house was perfect for the Szukas. It was almost 4,500 square feet, with five bedrooms, four bathrooms, handicapped accessible throughout, and high vaulted ceilings. Even before closing on the house was complete, the sellers gave permission to start remodeling.

Bruce handed Coni a large stack of floor plans and told her that she basically had 44 days to totally remodel and furnish this large home. It seemed an impossible task. But the more she prayed about it, the more she realized that she couldn't say no. The Szuka family, who had made so many personal sacrifices for their church and the special-needs ministry, were so deserving of a new house.

Coni left a quick message with some of her friends, asking them to pray that God would help her accomplish a special task with an almost impossible deadline.

Although Coni had received interior-design training, she definitely didn't feel adequate to lead such a venture in such a short time frame. But she took the first step: she shot lots of photos. They didn't have time to take exact measurements, except for the windows. Bruce's wife, Colleen, and her friend Tina joined Coni to help shop for the furniture and accessories. They were able to find about 80 percent of the furniture they needed from a store the donor had suggested.

During the next 11 days, Coni and her team worked around the clock, repainting the entire house, finding just the right furnishings and accessories, and assembling them all. The house had a key combo box on the door that allowed the volunteers to come and go as they had time.

Coni had no doubt that God had orchestrated the project; there were so many times when she had a need for the house and God would send just the volunteer she needed for a specialized task. For instance, she found a gigantic rug and needed someone to deliver it for her. She called a friend who owned a truck. He "just happened" to be with his son, who was tutored after school in the same shopping center, and was able to quickly deliver the rug to the house

On December 17, five days into the project, Coni picked up her close friend, Linda, from the airport. Linda owned her own design company. Coni had hesitated to tell Linda about the project because Linda had such a giving heart, and Coni didn't want her friend to feel obligated to volunteer. A gifted designer, Linda jumped right in to the project and made invaluable contributions on the final accessory selections and last-minute details.

On the tenth day, the night before their deadline, the house was filled with volunteers scurrying about doing last-minute details. Some volunteers even drove to Orlando to rent a moving truck and pick up the furniture. At 4:30 P.M., a big U-Haul truck pulled up with more than 100 large boxes of furniture that needed assembly. It was overwhelming. But another friend of Coni's, who was on surgical disability, had volunteered at the last minute to help in an advisory capacity. Much to Coni's surprise, she was on disability from a branch of the company they had ordered most of the furniture from. Amazingly, she already knew how to assemble and identify each piece of furniture. While she couldn't lift, she gave invaluable direction to the volunteers when they encountered problems putting everything together. Coni knew that it was only God who helped everything come together so nicely.

Volunteers ironed and hung window treatments; others made the beds with new sheets and bedspreads. Some mopped the floors and cleaned; others helped move furniture and add accessories. Even though they hadn't had time to measure, every piece of furniture fit just right. And despite almost two weeks of very late nights, none of the volunteers felt burdened, even though many of them were helping after their regular jobs. Even Coni, who was at the project more than full-time, felt amazingly energized. When Coni, Doug, Linda and Jill, who was also a huge help, finished after midnight, they vacuumed and prayed their way out of the house.

To get the Szuka family to the house on December 23, the church had scheduled their Special Needs Annual Christmas Party at the new house at 10:00 A.M. The Szukas had been told that a family named Smith (a fictional family) had volunteered their house for the party because it was large enough to hold all the people who were invited.

Alicia Szuka was impressed by the large house and wondered who owned it. One of the guests tried to get her to look at the master bedroom bathroom, but she declined to peek into someone else's bathroom.

More than 100 excited guests crowded into the main living area as Bruce Prevost got ready to make the surprise presentation. He gathered the Szuka family to the center of the room.

"Your family has served others time and again," Bruce began. "You have been an example to each of us . . ." After Bruce finished speaking, he handed Alicia Szuka the large ceremonial key to their new home.

Through tears of surprise and joy, Alicia graciously expressed that she felt so undeserving of this special gift. They had been praying for a home where they could better minister to people with special needs, so Alicia knew that God was the ultimate source of their new home, and that it had a greater purpose—to serve the needs of others.

Coni, Bruce and all of the other volunteers were so thankful that they had been the hands and feet of Jesus to this giving family. It was an inexpressible time of joy for all of them. As an added bonus, the volunteers all got their Christmas shopping and other responsibilities done in record time.

Unexpected blessings boomeranged back to my friend Coni too. Encouraged and cheered on by others, Coni and her friend Linda started the New Year by joining forces to launch their new design firm, Creative Concepts.

Christmas is most truly Christmas when we celebrate it
by giving the light of love to those who need it most.

—RUTH CARTER STAPLETON

My *Loved* Child,

Love one another because

I'm the *Source* of all love.
When you love, you know Me!
Challenge and *encourage* each other to
demonstrate love and good deeds.
Remember, even My Son wasn't born to be served.
He came to *serve*, and to *give* His life
as a ransom for many. Whatever you do,
do the *best job* you can. Work as if you're
doing it for Me. Remember that your
reward comes from Me and that you're
actually serving Me as you *serve others*.

Cheering You On,

YOUR GOD *of* LOVE

(1 John 4:7-8; Hebrews 10:24; Matthew 10:28; Colossians 3:23-24)

DEAREST CREATOR:

Thank You that You purposefully made me.
Help me make the most out of every opportunity
that You give me to serve others as we celebrate
Your Son's birthday. Forgive me for the times
when I feel inadequate—when You call me to step
out of my comfort zone. Remind me that when
I'm feeling weak, that's when You show up
to demonstrate Your power. I want to be an
ambassador of Your amazing love today, not just
at Christmas time but throughout the year.

My *Overwhelmed* Child,

Remember that children are

a *gift* and a *blessing* from Me!

You can trust Me to *faithfully provide*

anything your family needs according to

My endless *riches in glory.*

My divine power has already given you

everything

you need for *life* and *godliness.*

I've called you by My glory and goodness.

Graciously,

YOUR HEAVENLY FATHER

(Psalm 127:3; Philippians 4:19; 2 Peter 1:3)

Amazing
Providence

WHEN SHANTEL FOUND OUT she was pregnant, she felt a bit
overwhelmed. *"Lord, how am I going to manage raising five children under
the age of six, when it takes everything I have to raise the four little ones I
already have and love?"*

God graciously reminded Shantel that her children were a gift
from Him. She recalled the time, years earlier, when her doctor had
told her that she probably wouldn't be able to have children.
Amazingly, right after she fulfilled her obligation to the University
of Texas for her volleyball scholarship, she discovered that she was
pregnant with her and her husband, Josh's, first child, Caleb. And
there was little room to breathe between the next three births. It had
been a steady stream of wet diapers and sleepless nights. *What would
that doctor say now if she heard I was expecting my fifth child?* Reflecting
on the miraculous conceptions, she acknowledged that
the little one inside her, due to arrive on December 25,
would also be a special Christmas present from
God to their family.

Shantel's husband, three-time Olympic
Gold Medalist Josh Davis, was still under
the U.S. Swim Team's medical insurance.

While the pay for national athletes isn't enough to sustain a family, the medical benefits are superb. Josh's insurance through the team covered all his family's medical expenses with a small $40 copay and no deductible; however, his eligibility for insurance was scheduled to end on December 31.

Since Shantel's actual due date for the newest Davis baby was Christmas Day, Josh and Shantel didn't think there would be any problem when they applied for new coverage with an independent company. There would only be a one-week gap before their new insurance coverage started in early January.

Shantel delivered Liam on December 18. The whole family was excited about their early Christmas present. When they brought Liam home, he caught a little cold that was going around the Davis household. Shantel had taken Liam to the doctor for his checkup, and the doctor was treating his respiratory problem. But on Christmas Eve, Shantel noticed that Liam was struggling to breathe. They took him to the hospital where he was diagnosed with respiratory syncytial virus (RSV). RSV isn't necessarily a big deal for adults, but it can be very serious for a little baby.

When they admitted Liam to the intensive care unit, Shantel thought to herself, *I hope it won't be a long stay, because we only have medical coverage until the end of the year.* But as the New Year approached, Liam remained in intensive care and the bills continued to mount.

The U.S. Swim Team does have some discretionary provision to make a special request for wild-card coverage for swimmers no longer meeting eligibility criteria. So Josh called them and asked about the possibility of extending his medical coverage for another week. He understood when his request was denied.

Liam was finally released from the hospital on January 3. During those extra three days, he had racked up additional medical bills totaling over $20,000, which weren't eligible for insurance coverage. Josh and Shantel weren't sure how they were going to pay the bills, but they were just grateful that their baby was finally coming home again.

Miraculously, the U.S. Swim Team called back and told Josh that they had reconsidered. They relayed how much they appreciated all he had done to promote the sport of swimming. Not only did they pay Liam's entire medical bill, but they also covered the Davis family's insurance for an entire additional year. There was no doubt in Josh's and Shantel's minds that this reversal was a gift from God with an extra bonus of continued coverage.

My friend Adam introduced me to the Davis family when Liam was still a baby, and an instant bond of friendship started. Their home in San Antonio has become a favorite hangout for me. Shantel, Josh, Caleb, Abby, Luke, Annie and Liam have truly been blessings from God in my life. When Shantel recounted this testimony of God's faithfulness, she said, "It's so easy to say you believe that God will provide all your needs, but when you are facing a desperate need, and God supernaturally intervenes on your behalf, you really come to *know* Him as your Jehovah Jireh. It was such a faith booster to see God truly provide."

My *Treasured* Child,

Look up and remember that *your help* comes from Me! Remember that I Am your sufficiency. Because I *love* you, you are *more* than an overcomer. Things that are *impossible* on your own become *possible* with Me. I can even change a king's heart. You can always count on My great *faithfulness* and *compassion*. May you experience My *renewing loving* kindness each morning.

Faithfully,

YOUR JEHOVAH JIREH

(Your Provider)

(Psalm 121:1-2, 2 Corinthians 3:5, Romans 8:37, Luke 18:27, Proverbs 21:1, Lamentations 3:22-23)

HEAVENLY FATHER,

I want to please You by trusting You instead of worrying about the future. Help me look to You for all my needs and for my family's needs. Remind me that N O T H I N G is too difficult for You, even if it seems impossible to me. Thank You for Your promise that You'll provide E V E R Y T H I N G I need—emotionally, physically or financially. Encourage me with the promises of Your Word. Help me truly know You as my Jehovah Jireh. Thanks that I can count on Your faithfulness and creativity for solutions that go far beyond all that I can ask or dream. Your love amazes me!

My *Disappointed* Child,

Draw **near** to Me with *confidence!*

Come **boldly** before My throne of *grace.*

You'll find ***overflowing mercy*** in your

time of **need**. Even when your spirit is

overwhelmed and grows faint within you,

I always know *the way* for you!

I'll **satisfy** the *longings* of your soul

and **fill** you with My *goodness.*

Let My *gladness* and **joy** overtake you!

My Forever *Love,*

YOUR FAITHFUL FRIEND *and* GUIDE

(Hebrews 4:16; Psalm 142:3; Psalm 107:9; Isaiah 54:11)

Rainbow
Promises

FOR YEARS, RICK'S CHRISTMASES had grown progressively worse as his wife, Debbie, battled an undiagnosed illness. Right before Thanksgiving, Rick and Debbie moved back to northern New Mexico, with Rick's high hopes that the climate of the Rocky Mountain West would help restore his wife's health. They were encouraged when at last doctors determined that Debbie needed a liver transplant and she was cleared to start the process to be placed on the donor waiting list. Before that could happen, their hopes were dashed again when Debbie went to the hospital for another surgical procedure and contracted double pneumonia.

As Debbie's health rapidly deteriorated, Rick helplessly watched his wife literally starving to death. Her doctors couldn't figure out what was wrong. Three weeks before Christmas 2005, Debbie underwent procedures to discover why her body wasn't able to digest food anymore.

With the threat of even greater expenses from more medical procedures and the possibility of a liver transplant, Debbie had decided they shouldn't exchange Christmas gifts. But Rick wondered how many more Christmases he would be able to share with his loving wife, and so he searched for the perfect gifts. He found an antique rose-colored crystal perfume dispenser, because Debbie had recently begun collecting perfume bottles. He also bought her jewelry and a brilliant rainbow-colored bookmark, knowing that rainbows were significant to his wife, as they always symbolized their hope for God's healing. Debbie surprised Rick with a retro Atari game system, and they greatly enjoyed a few hours playing Pong (even when Debbie beat him every game).

Knowing that Debbie couldn't eat anything, Rick had a cold-cut sandwich for his Christmas dinner in lieu of cooking the organic turkey he had specially ordered. They discussed returning to the emergency room, but Debbie insisted on staying home. She was tired of continual medical procedures and tests with-out answers or results. They couldn't even celebrate the purchase of their new home. The living room was still piled with boxes from the move. Together they found solace in watching a few Christmas movies and thinking of distant memories of happier Christmases past.

With his family and friends more than 42 hours away, Rick felt alone as he watched his wife sleep through much of the holidays. It was obvious that she was getting weaker. He wondered what their future held. The God he loved and trusted seemed so distant at this time of Rick's greatest need. *Would Debbie live to receive the liver transplant that offered hope for a cure, or would this be their last Christmas together?*

Little did Rick know that his hopes for Debbie's physical healing were about to be shattered. A month after Christmas, exploratory surgery revealed the presence of cancer that was untreatable and inoperable. The doctors offered no hope. It was only a matter of time before she passed away. All Rick could hold on to was a faint hint of God's presence and promises.

That first autumn after Debbie's death, Rick drove to the post office. As he walked inside, he looked up and saw a thunderstorm rolling off the mountains. A bright rainbow at the leading edge of the storm caught his eye. For one brief moment, hope and joy welled up in Rick. He reflected on the rainbows of hope that Debbie had so often experienced while battling her illness. He was reminded of his former intimacy with God.

As a widower now, the rainbow suddenly became a harsh reminder of lost love, crushed hopes and shattered dreams. Remembering Debbie's pain and suffering, Rick silently told God, "Forget it! Right now, I don't want to hurt anymore. I've had it up to here with Your bogus rainbows and hollow promises. You didn't heal Debbie when we trusted You for a cure."

Rick returned to his truck and drove home, heading into the dark storm clouds and venting some storm clouds of his own in the form of anger toward God. The strength of his emotions surprised him. He had bottled up his feelings for months just trying to survive. But as he honestly spilled out his guts to God, Rick's emotions moved from anger to a flood of tears of disappointment and abandonment. He felt such a release as he sobbed before God. Rick poured out his hurt, expressing his sorrow and loneliness, and questioning why God had taken Debbie away from him.

Driving farther north into the storm clouds, more rainbows appeared in the sky. It was as if his prayers were being led by the rainbows. He noticed a strangely shaped rainbow that looked like a door. God gently reminded Rick that He had given Debbie a new body and she no longer suffered pain. Unlike Rick, she no longer had tears. That first rainbow symbolized Debbie and was quickly fading away into the cloudy darkness beyond. It seemed as if the rainbows were interacting with his prayers, and God was showing him something. It was a clear time of communication between Rick and God. Rick was brutally honest and God was tenderly truthful.

As Rick expressed his doubt that God would ever be able to fill that empty place in his heart left by Debbie's death, just to the west of the fading rainbow, on the other side of the road, another similarly shaped but brightly vivid and larger rainbow appeared. Just like the clean mountain showers outside, Rick felt an unexpected and refreshing release from the broken dreams of his past. He felt his desperate sorrow, hopelessness, loneliness and hidden bitterness leaving him as God flooded him with a startling new hope. Rick realized that this brighter rainbow symbolized God's promise that someone else was waiting for him, and he wouldn't be alone.

Rick couldn't ignore the bright hope that God showed him, and he sure didn't let God forget it as he daily reminded Him of that promise. Rick started anticipating, expecting and praying for the person God would bring into his life.

Right before Thanksgiving, he started corresponding with a Christian woman from Orlando, Florida, with whom he was matched online through e-Harmony.

That woman was me.

In December 2006, we had an opportunity to meet face to face for the first time.

After hearing Rick's story, I knew that Christmas was a time for Rick to rebuild his relationship with his boys. Two prodigal sons had returned home, and all three of his sons were home with him for the first Christmas in many years. Rick was still grieving Debbie's death, but he was starting to heal.

Our relationship grew throughout the following year. Rick invited me to come spend Christmas 2007 with his family. After flying into Albuquerque, we drove to Santa Fe. Rick took me back to the restaurant inside the historical LaFonda. We asked to be seated at the same table in front of the fireplace where we had eaten dinner while on our first date a year and three days earlier. After the waitress took our order, Rick prayed a word of blessing over our time together, and we talked.

As we waited for our meal, I wondered where our relationship was headed. Rick had been unusually distant and edgy all day. He just wasn't himself and seemed somewhat preoccupied. Although we had talked in October about the possibility of marriage, I secretly wondered if Rick was getting cold feet and planned to break up with me. Then he unexpectedly reached into his pocket and delicately slid a small red box across the table.

Rick tells me that I had a deer-in-the-headlights look on my face. As I said, "Honey, what's this?" he noticed a tear form in my eye.

I opened the box and stared at the beautiful diamond ring that Rick and I had admired at my friend Virginia Ann's jewelry store in Orlando a few months earlier. For once in my life, I was speechless. I knew there was a remote possibility that he might propose to me on Christmas or on Valentine's Day, but it never crossed my mind that he was going to propose that night. I had missed the clue when he prayed, "God, bless this special occasion." I thought he was just blessing our first anniversary of dating.

Rick interrupted the silence by saying, "Honey, I would get down on my knee, but I see a Three Stooges episode with me floundering on this beautifully waxed floor; then you falling as you try to help me up. And then we both set off a domino effect of tumbling chairs, china, tables . . . I think I'd better avoid the slapstick and leave this romantic moment untarnished by remaining seated."

I couldn't hold back my tears of joy as Rick continued, "Seriously, LeAnn, I love you and want to spend the rest of my life with you. Will you marry me?"

After I said, "I've been waiting for you for a long time. Of course I'll marry you! I love you too," Rick slid the ring on my finger and then lovingly clasped my hands in his. After admiring the ring on my hand and silently practicing the name LeAnn Weiss-Rupard, I stood up and reached across our small table to kiss my future husband.

When the waitress returned to the table, I held out my left hand so that she couldn't miss seeing the sparkling ring on my finger. Eyeing the small red box and the beaming smile on my face, she congratulated us and took our picture. Rick recalls that I showed off my ring to every guest in the restaurant and later in the town square as we walked in the chilly night air enjoying the colorful Christmas lights and light blanket of snow.

I didn't care if I received any other present for Christmas. Rick was the only present I really wanted. I'd waited more than four decades for my future husband. During those long years of waiting, my friends often encouraged me that God was spending extra time preparing a special man for me. But I'll admit that sometimes it actually seemed like my heavenly Father had plumb forgotten that one desire of my heart.

During much of the last few years of my waiting, Rick was suffering through devastating trials as God refined him. But in His perfect timing, God caused our paths to cross even though we lived more than half a map away from each other. Now we both share an exciting expectancy of serving God and others together.

If you're experiencing disappointments this Christmas, be reminded that God is seldom early, but He's never late. As you wait, be assured that God sees the entire puzzle and is working behind the scenes for you, even when you can't feel His presence. That's what faith is all about.

Shake the dust from your past, and move forward in His promises.

— KAY ARTHUR

My *Lonely* Child,

Even when things aren't meeting your *expectations* and *plans,* know that I will fulfill My purposes for your life! My love for you endures forever. I'll *never abandon* you! Leave the baggage of your past behind. See that I'm doing a NEW thing! I will even make a way in your driest wilderness seasons of life. Watch Me *bring life* to what you thought was wasteland. You can't begin to imagine all of the *wonderful* things I've prepared for you because you love Me.

Dreaming for you,

YOUR ALL-POWERFUL FATHER

(Psalm 138:8; Matthew 19:26; Isaiah 43:18-19; 1 Corinthians 2:9)

53

DEAREST FATHER,

I confess to You that I've been in a dry time in my relationship with You, and I'm desperate for You. Sometimes I'm disappointed when You don't choose to direct my life the way I hoped You would.

But You're a creative God, and You work in different ways. I acknowledge that Your ways are so much higher than my ways. Please help me release anything from my past that is stopping me from becoming everything You created me to be. Make me passionate for You! Open my eyes to the dreams and possibilities You have awaiting me. I need You! Remind me that only You can satisfy the longings of my heart. Help me patiently wait for You! And when it's time to take action, help me move forward in Your abundant promises.

My *Beloved* Child,

Catch a glimpse of My *incredible* an

indescribable love just for you. . . .

I *pray* that you, being rooted and

established in love, may have power to grasp how

wide and *long* and *high* and *deep*

is My totally unconditional love for YOU! My

love for you incomparably *surpasses* all human

knowledge of love. May you be filled with the

fullness of God.

My Everlasting *Love,*

J E S U S

(Ephesians 3:17-19)

christmas eve intruders

THE BREAK-IN HAPPENED back in 1936, when the Great Depression was still paralyzing the land. Nine-year-old Charlie Jones, the oldest of five children, and his family had relocated from Alabama to Lancaster County, Pennsylvania, where his father had somehow managed to rent a little row house.

As Christmas approached, Charlie's dad realized that he had nothing extra to spend on Christmas presents for his small children. In desperation, he had gone to the bank to try to convince the banker that he was a safe risk for a small loan.

"I don't have a job or any collateral," Mr. Jones shared with the banker, "but I'm a hard worker, and my five children will be tremendously disappointed without any Christmas."

The banker had to decline Mr. Jones's loan application, but he proposed a creative alternative to Charlie's father. "Mr. Jones, I wish I could grant your request; unfortunately, I can't. A lot of people in this town are in a similar predicament. But I have an idea. If you can postpone celebrating Christmas by a day or two, all the prices will be reduced in the stores and you would only need half as much as you are requesting. If this proposal is agreeable to you, I could approve a loan for a smaller amount."

Mr. Jones shook the banker's hand, gratefully accepting the offer. Better to give his children a late Christmas than no Christmas at all.

On Christmas Eve, Charlie and his family were tucked in their beds when the front door suddenly slammed open—people didn't lock their doors at night the way we do today. There was a commotion of noise and footsteps downstairs. Charlie's dad rushed down the stairs to discover what was happening; maybe intruders were trying to steal the little they had!

After a few minutes had passed, Charlie carefully ventured downstairs to make sure his father was okay. He found his father sitting on the bottom step of the stairs with his face buried in his hands. *Why was his dad weeping?*

As Charlie reached the bottom step, he noticed that the hallway was lined with boxes of food, clothing and candy. He couldn't miss seeing the big red fire engine waiting to be ridden, or the four-foot-wide folding dollhouse for his sisters.

Needless to say, it was a Christmas that was always remembered by Charlie's family. They never learned who the gracious intruders were. It was somewhat of a mystery, because all of their friends were as poor as they were, and Charlie's parents didn't go to church, although they sent him and his siblings to Sunday school.

But Charlie's dad always had a "prime suspect" in mind. When he returned to the bank to repay the loan, the kind banker had said, "I'm sorry, Mr. Jones, but I don't have any record on file of a loan to you."

Of all of the wonderful Christmases that Charlie has ever experienced, that Christmas during the Great Depression remains one of his favorites, although he didn't fully understand the experience until years later—after he had confessed the truth of John 3:16 and understood the significance of God's greatest gift to the world, and Jesus became his Lord and Savior.

That's when Charlie also realized that he had been blessed to see God's love in action through the generosity of some of His children. He realized that those unknown intruders were God's servants practicing the words of 1 John 3:16:

> Hereby perceive we the love of God, because he laid down his life for us: and we ought to lay down our lives for the brethren (*KJV*).

In time, Charlie became nationally known as Tremendous Charlie Jones. For more than 60 years, this top motivational speaker and author has passed on the kindness shown to him when he was nine years old by spreading humor, encouragement and his trademark hugs. Charlie never meets a stranger, and he has given away countless books to encourage others to read. For decades, Charlie has invited poor children to his home, a large estate featuring an amusement park. Over the years, thousands of children have been blessed and entertained by his stories, the amusement park rides, snow cones, hot dogs and Christmas carols year-round, thanks to Charlie's tremendous love.

What makes you different from the person you'll be in five years is the books you've read and the people you've met.

—TREMENDOUS JONES

My *Blessed* Child,

I demonstrated real love by laying down

My life for you. Follow My example

and *sacrifice* yourself for others by loving

them with the same *care* and *concern*

that you have for yourself.

I show My love to a thousand generations

of those who love Me and keep

My commandments. Surely My *goodness*

and unfailing kindness will surround

you and follow you each and *every day*

of your life.

Loving You Always,

YOUR REASON FOR THE SEASON

(1 John 3:16; Leviticus 19:18; Deuteronomy 5:10; Psalm 23:6)

DEAREST LORD,

You are a good God. You know what I need even before I ask. I can always count on Your faithfulness and kindness. Thank You for Your promise that Your goodness and love will always bless me. Help me pass on Your love to others. May love be a trademark of my life so that people will know that I follow You.

My *Hopeful* Child,

Never forget that I'm *for you!*

I'm 100 percent faithful

to all of My *promises* to you.

You can always count on Me

and My love for you. Even the seemingly

impossible things in your life

become possibilities with Me.

Guiding You,

YOUR EVER-FAITHFUL GOD

(Romans 8:31; Psalm 145:13; Matthew 19:2)

Maybe you need a Christmas miracle. To be pregnant with the hope of the impossible. To have relationships restored. Dreams renewed. Hurts healed. Hearts comforted. To see God with you in a real way.

—KARLA DORNACHER

promises FulFilled

SANDY, WHO LIVED IN St. Paul, Minnesota, had just finished her Master's thesis and was seeking God for direction for the next phase of her life. She hoped it would include marriage. She decided to study the life of Abraham in the Bible because he was a friend of God and lived by faith, and Sandy wanted that to be true in her life as well. Her journal records her inspirational journey of faith as she trusted God to fulfill His promise to give her a family.

Monday, September 27, 1974, at 11:45 P.M., Sandy wrote in her journal:

> *Father God—*
> *I just got a jolt!! After writing to You,*
> *I got my Bible,* The Berkeley Version, *and waited on You to know where to read. Abraham came to mind because, thinking of the doors to be opened through finishing my paper, and thinking to the unknown of next summer, I feel a little like he did, starting out on a new venture ("I make all things new").*

*I felt I should turn to Genesis 15, so I did. When I reached verse 4, I was startled, shocked, and amazed. These words pierced through to my inner being — "Then the Lord's message to him was . . . **your heir will be born from your own body.**"*

I wait on You for Your will, and my soul doth magnify Your holy name. Amen and Amen.

Sandy had enjoyed a successful career as a teacher and as a principal of an experimental school. But she was excited by the belief that God was promising her that she would have a baby, which she also understood to imply the promise of a husband. Although Sandy had learned to be content with her singleness, marriage and children were strong desires of her heart.

On October 18, Sandy turned 32. Even though she was beautiful, at that time in our culture, she was already at, or rapidly approaching, "old maid" status. Most of her close friends had been married for years. Sandy didn't even have any dating prospects, much less marriage prospects.

Friday, November 26, 1974, she wrote:

Lord Jesus, I really am anticipating the partner You have for me. Please send him soon if it pleases You. Now that I have the assurance that it is in Your will for me to marry, I would like to marry soon and have my children before I get much older. These are the deep and growing desires of my heart.

However, my will is yielded to You if this is not Your will yet. I look to You to know You, rest in You, and please You.

Thank You for hearing, listening, and caring. I love You.
Amen

On October 20, 1972, Sandy sensed that God was opening her heart to consider a new possibility of marrying a widower, and wrote:

Dear Lord Jesus,

As I've thought about being married, I've always pictured someone who has never been married before. Tonight, however, the thought has come (through reading an article in the newspaper) that perhaps You may not only want me to marry a widower, but one with a child or children. My heart and mind are open to You regarding this possibility, dear Savior, for the first time. With Your help and the assurance of Your will, I am willing to marry a widower with or without a family.

Wherever my beloved is, bless, keep, and guide him. Enfold him in Your love, and bring us together soon, I pray.

Thank You, Jesus.

Amen.

On October 23, 1972, at 8:30 P.M., Sandy sensed an urgency to pray for her future husband:

Dear Lord Jesus,

There is a great urgency in my heart to pray for my loved one—not just of myself, but I feel prompted by You. I feel it will not be long before we meet. Guide my steps. Guide his steps. Open the door for us to meet. I'm reminded of the words in Jeremiah 33:3: "Call unto Me, and I will answer thee, and show thee great and mighty things, which thou knowest not."

Lord Jesus, I'm calling unto You for my loved one. Thank You for Your promise. Thank You now for listening. I love You.

Amen.

For some time Sandy had felt that God might be preparing her to marry a man in the ministry. She closed with a passage from the book *Hind's Feet on*

High Places that she had been reading that night. On Sunday, November 9, 1972, at 11:15 P.M., Sandy reflected:

> *Dear Lord Jesus,*
>
> *What am I to think? For some time I've told You about my desire and/or willingness to marry a man in the ministry. Last month You dealt with me regarding my willingness to marry a widower with or without children, and I said I was willing. I've also expressed a deep desire to meet this person this fall.*
>
> *Last Thursday night, when I came home from seeing* Fiddler on the Roof *with Heidi, Jan had a note for me saying that a pastor had called long distance who wanted to stop in to see my preschool. He said I didn't know him, and he didn't know me.*
>
> *Well, he came to school Friday around 3:30 P.M., and I showed him around, gave him some copies of the materials list, objectives, and an extra catalog from Saint Paul Book and Stationery. Then he related why he'd come and asked if he could take me out to dinner.*
>
> *We stopped here at the apartment and then went to Mr. Steak near Rosedale. He told of losing his wife in a car accident in August. He has four children 9, 6, 4 and 3. He shared some about his ministry . . . .*
>
> *P.S. "My Lord, may I ask one thing? Is the time at last soon coming when You will fulfill the promise that You gave me?"*
>
> *He said very gently, yet with great joy, "Yes — the time is not long now. Dare to begin to be happy. If you will go forward in the way before you, you will soon receive the promise, and I will give you your heart's desire. It is not long . . ."* Hind's Feet on High Places, *page 121. Dare to begin to be happy.*

I, LeAnn, am the six-year-old child in this story. My mother, JoAnn, had been killed in a car accident on August 26, 1972. I was next to the oldest of my three siblings.

A long-distance courtship started between my dad, Pastor Lee Weiss, and Sandy, rotating between St. Paul, Minnesota, and LaCrosse, Wisconsin. On January 25, 1973, my dad asked Sandy to become his wife.

The next day, we met our future mom, Sandra J. Martens, for the first time. Many of the promises that God gave Sandy, as recorded in her journal, were fulfilled when she married my dad on March 24, 1973.

That fall, we moved to Florida. Sandy accepted us as her own children and eventually adopted us. We never considered her to be a stepmother; she was our mom. In fact, I was blessed with two great moms. Mom (Sandy) told us she felt that God had promised her that she would have a baby. We were all excited about the prospect of another brother or sister.

After Mom and Dad had been married several years, a couple came to visit us at our large ministry home. The wife asked my mom if she had any biological children with my dad. My mom shared that they had been trying to have a baby. The visitor shared that God had given her a ministry of praying for women who had never conceived, and she felt impressed to pray for my mom. She laid a hand on Mom's head and the other on Mom's waist as she prayed.

Afterwards, she told my mom, "I sense that God will give you a child, but not right away."

Again, we were excited about the prospect of a baby. As the years passed, we continued to pray that Mom would have a baby. But our hope faded as Mom grew older. On Mom's fortieth birthday, she sensed that she would have the baby God had promised before her next birthday.

December 15, 1979, Mom was rereading accounts relating the Christmas story, when Isaiah 9:6 spoke to her heart. When she read, "Unto us a child is born . . ." she *knew* that she was pregnant days before it could be medically verified. She kept the revelation a secret.

Instant pregnancy tests hadn't been invented yet. The first day that Mom could take a test that would be valid was December 25, 1979. On Christmas Day, we thought we had opened all of our presents. But Mom said, "Wait, I think there's one more present."

Mom brought out a small stocking. As one of us opened it, we discovered a baby Jesus inside and wondered what the gift meant. We read the clue, "Unto us a child is born." Mom was always giving us spiritual applications, whether we wanted them or not, so we waited for her explanation.

She came back holding the pregnancy test, which revealed pink for positive, and explained that we were finally going to have our promised baby. That was the best present we could ask for. It was a Christmas full of joy at our house. The good news quickly spread to the other families who lived with us.

Then my dad recounted another Christmas story from years earlier. When Dad had married my birth mom, JoAnn, they tried for several years to get pregnant without any success. Then, at Christmas in 1962, there was a huge box under the tree with my grandparents' names on it. When it came time to open the gifts, my grandparents didn't want to open it until my mom was there to watch. But my dad insisted they open it first. When they unwrapped the big box and opened the lid, my mom jumped out wearing a "Mommy" bib and gave my dad a "Daddy" bib. That's when everyone learned that my oldest sister, Pat, was on the way. It was a big deal with lots of celebration, as she was the first grandchild on both the Weiss and Allen sides of our family.

Back to Christmas 1979. We were all excited about the long-awaited announcement of our promised baby. Mom was sure it was going to be a boy and picked out the name Matthew Lee. Because of Mom's age, doctors wanted her to take a test to see if the baby had Down's syndrome. But mom refused. Abortion was never an option. We would love the baby God had promised, no matter what.

We all enjoyed preparing for our brother. We surprised my mom with a special baby shower. On August 18, my mom went into labor. Dad later rushed to the hospital. We anxiously waited for a call (cell phones hadn't been invented yet). Hours later, Dad finally called us to ask us to pray. Both the baby and my mom were in distress. The umbilical cord was wrapped around the baby's neck, and they were rushing Mom into surgery for an emergency C-section.

The doctor had forgotten to come out and tell my dad that everything had gone okay. So my dad waited another hour thinking that my mom or the baby, or both, had died.

It seemed like an eternity before my dad called to tell us that we had a new baby. August 19, 1980, God finally fulfilled the promise that He had made to my mom almost nine years earlier. The ultimate surprise was that Matthew Lee was actually a baby sister. My mom had been so sure that the baby was a boy that my parents hadn't even discussed a girl's name. So my youngest sister, Sarah Lee, was called Baby Weiss for several days.

Shortly after Sarah was born, my oldest sister, Pat, left home for Stetson University. I didn't seem to mind changing lots of diapers and baby-sitting during my last years of high school. My brother, Steve, and sister, Sharon, also pitched in.

Sarah has been a joy to our family and is now serving the Lord in Kenya, East Africa, with her husband and children, Victoria and David, alongside my parents. She's a talented singer. Her birth was a reminder to me that God always keeps His promises, even if His timing may be much later than we wanted.

Never doubt in the dark what God told you in the light.
– V. RAYMOND EDMAN

My *Persevering* Child,

Don't quit. Cling to the hope

that you profess without wavering,

because I'm faithful to My promises.

Don't lose heart in *doing good.*

You will be rewarded at the

right time if you press on when you're

tempted to stop. Even when you backslide

and lack faith, I'm always faithful.

Sustaining You,

TRUSTWORTHY GOD

(Hebrews 10:23; Galatians 6:9; 2 Timothy 2:13)

The Spirit of Christmas

- Think about instances in your life when you or a loved one had a need and God met that need. Thank God for His faithfulness.

- Write a note to God about a current need that's causing you anxiety. Date your letter and save it as a testimony to you when God answers. Search the Bible for promises that correspond to your need. (You can look up applicable key words using Bible Software.)

DEAR FATHER,

Sometimes it's easy to doubt You when it doesn't seem like You're answering my prayers within my limited time frame. I confess that delays often frustrate me. Forgive me for being impatient. Lord, remind me of Your faithfulness in my life. Thank You that You're always dependable, even when I'm not faithful to You.

Don't let my faith waiver when I'm disappointed.

I want to trust in Your promises wholeheartedly.

Help me meditate on Your Word so that I'll remember Your promises when the enemy tries to distract me.

I love You and praise You for being trustworthy.

My *Made-for-Relationship* Child,

I give you *patience* and *encouragement*

to help you live in complete harmony and

unity with each other. Be devoted to

your family and friends in brotherly love,

honoring others above yourself.

Watch what you say. Use your words to

build others up according to their need.

Let your words benefit others this season.

Praise Me, united together to give *all glory* to Me

Bringing Peace to Your Holiday,

YOUR LOVING FATHER

(Romans 15:5-6; Ephesians 4:29; Romans 12:10)

Family Ties

IN SO MANY OF THE CHRISTMAS film classics, the holidays are a wonderful showcase of near-perfect family get-togethers. Almost everyone pitches in to bring something for the family dinner. Remember the heartfelt prayers and attitude of gratitude of Charles Ingalls, on the TV family drama *Little House on the Prairie?* And what about *The Waltons?* Think about the bustle of pleasant conversation and laughter around the Christmas table surrounded by four generations of Waltons. Remember how they all worked together until the last dish was handwashed? And who can forget the soothing narrative of John Boy after everyone cheerfully said goodnight in unison? Or the joyous turnaround of George Bailey (played by Jimmy Stewart) in the film *It's a Wonderful Life?*

Today, with families spread out across the country, with the growing expense of travel due to rising gas prices, the complications of blended families, dealing with in-laws and "out-laws" and rotating child custody for holidays, the gap between desire and reality can often be crushing.

Just ask my friend. I'll call her Elizabeth to protect her family. Years ago, her children were devastated when their dad committed suicide while they were at home. Later, Elizabeth remarried and dealt with a blended family situation. There was a series of catastrophic events mixed in with normal family squabbles. Hurts were buried and never dealt with. Several of her children didn't stay connected to their faith, which resulted in quite a difference in core values among family members.

Between not dealing with past emotional wounds, personality differences and busyness, family priorities slowly deteriorated over time and family relationships drifted. As the children began to move out on their own, Christmas dinners were often disappointing.

Due to a serious issue, some family members barely talked with other members, despite Elizabeth's earnest attempts at mediation. If one found the other was coming for Christmas, that family member would cancel. Some holidays one or more kids had committed to spend Christmas with friends or in-laws, or said they had to work. Elizabeth wondered if they were just giving excuses to avoid dealing with past hurts. One of her greatest desires was to have her family all together again without the usual strife.

One year, Elizabeth and her husband, Peter, were asked to star as the parents in the church Christmas musical. Ironically, the plot of the musical revolved around excitement over all of the children coming home for Christmas.

Wouldn't that be special if our entire family could be together again, Elizabeth prayed, as she acted out the scene. That Christmas, God answered Elizabeth's prayer. She had invited all of the kids to the musical, and they all came. She couldn't believe it when all of their children and their spouses came home. They exchanged presents and had a cordial dinner, gathering around the table. It was a real joy for Elizabeth to see her family focusing on each other. They even had a special family picture taken that captured a family memory she'll always cherish.

If your family isn't picture perfect, you're in good company. It takes extra effort to keep family relationships in good order; but it's well worth everything you sacrifice to make family a priority and make good memories together, especially during the holidays. God created us for relationship. We need each other.

My *Child,*

Relationships matter. Give the *gift* of mercy
this Christmas. Be kind, humble, gentle
and patient. *Get along* with each other and
forgive each other. When someone wrongs you,
forgive him, just as Christ *forgives you.*
Don't forget that love is the most important
gift you can give. Love holds you all *together*
in perfect unity. Let My peace rule in your hearts
this holiday and *throughout* the year.
Let My Word guide you as you teach and
challenge each other. May an *attitude*
of gratitude toward Me invade your environment.
Utilize *wisdom* and *understanding*
to build your family.

Love,
YOUR LORD *of* PEACE

(Colossians 3:12-17; Proverbs 24:3-4)

« 73 »

HEAVENLY FATHER,

The holidays tend to bring out the best and worst in people. Please use my voice to bring life to those I interact with this Christmas. Don't let my words break anyone's spirit. Let my life be an instrument of peace to others. Help me guard my words so that I won't escalate conflicts.

Give me Your wisdom to listen to and understand the hidden needs of those who cross my path. Help me make sacrifices for others and be patient with them like You're always patient with me. I want to be a light for You this Christmas and throughout the year.

My *Tested* Child,

Although you're squeezed by trouble on *every* side, you're not crushed or broken. Despite your unanswered *"Whys?"* you haven't quit or given up. I promise that I'll never *abandon* you or *destroy* you. *Joyfully reflect* on the benefits your current trials are producing. Realize that the testing of your faith is building your patience level. Remember that I'm strengthening you so that you'll be able to *endure* and *finish*. And don't forget the bonus: I'm making you mature and complete so that you will lack nothing.

My Pure *Joy*,

YOUR HEAVENLY FATHER

(2 Corinthians 4:8-9; James 1:2-4)

Joy is a by-product not of happy circumstances, education or talent,
but of a healthy relationship with God and a determination to love Him
no matter what. —BARBARA JOHNSON

Lessons in
True Joy

PEARL HARBOR DAY, December 7, 1999, is a day that will always live in the memory of the Murk family. It's a day that forever changed their lives. Heather and her father, Bill, suffering from lingering bronchitis, left their house to visit their doctor and run some other errands. They had the right of way and were waved through a one-way construction work zone by the flagman. The last thing Bill remembers is seeing a semi truck speeding toward them, and bracing for the impact.

After the head-on collision, somehow Bill managed to dial home on his cell phone. "Jeanine, we've been in a bad accident," he reported to his wife.

"Where are you?" Jeanine asked, frantic from hearing her daughter's screams in the background.

In shock, he responded simply, "I don't know."

Then the phone went dead.

Mrs. Murk and her daughter Brienne did the only thing they could. They prayed, hoping that the phone would ring again. A few minutes later, the phone did ring. This time it was a police officer telling them where the accident was and urging Mrs. Murk to hurry.

In their rush to get to the scene, they accidentally locked the keys in the van and had to find a neighbor to drive them. By the time they arrived, Heather had already been taken away in the ambulance. But when Mrs. Murk saw a huge pool of blood were her daughter had been, she knew that they had to rush to the hospital immediately.

Looking back, the delay was probably a God-thing. They didn't need to be driving in their condition, and it also gave the emergency team a head start on cleaning up Heather before they saw her. Still, nothing prepared Brienne and her mom for what they would see.

Bill Murk had looked like a pretzel when the paramedics extracted him from the van. Both of his hips had been crushed. At the hospital, he was in traction flat on his back. Heather's face had been lacerated with glass and was almost unrecognizable. The doctors reported that she had one of the worst cases of head trauma they had ever seen. The plastic surgeon who was called in put 450 stitches in Heather's face alone. He also was able to save her tongue, which was 95 percent severed in the back. All of Heather's major organs were badly bruised. And she couldn't talk. But amazingly, she didn't have any broken bones.

Heather's left eye had been pierced through the cornea with glass. Several days after the accident, a doctor realized that no eye doctor had reviewed her case. Immediately an eye specialist was summoned. When he examined her eye, the specialist was irate, commenting, "This child has had glass go through the cornea of her eye. At the very least she should have been rushed in for emergency laser eye surgery." Now, examining Heather's eyes, he became more and more perplexed as he said, "Are you sure no one else has touched her eye? Because the glass has been removed, and the surgery has been completed perfectly, but not by a human hand." Amazingly, Heather now has 20/20 vision, and she didn't before the accident.

Heather didn't remember much the first week after the accident, except the intolerable pain. Even the morphine drip she received every six minutes couldn't dull the pain. Just having the sheets touching her skin was excruciating.

The day after the accident, Mrs. Murk looked in on her 12-year-old daughter, wondering what her future held. The previous day, the doctors had given her a prognosis that her daughter would never speak or sing again. Not only was she a professional singer, but also their entire family sang together, and the girls represented a seventh generation of full-time music ministry for their family. But more important, she knew that singing was also her daughter's greatest expression of worship to God. As a mom, she couldn't take that hope away from Heather, so she kept silent about the prognosis.

Now the doctor was offering a small possibility that Heather might be able to talk again after a few years of intense therapy, but he thought it highly unlikely that Heather would be able to sing again.

As Mrs. Murk looked in on her daughter, Heather's eyes were still swollen shut. Her face was the size of a football. The song "The Prayer," sung by Celine Dion, came on the TV in Heather's room. Heather desperately wanted to sing along, but she felt entombed and trapped. She couldn't escape her body. She could barely even cry. It was as if she were experiencing a living death. There were several times when the pain was almost unbearable. At those times, Heather just prayed that God would take her home to be with Jesus.

When Heather's mom looked over and saw her daughter's throat moving as she tried to sing, she had to turn away to hide her tears.

When Celine sang another line of the song, Heather kept trying to sing too. All of a sudden, a small echo came out. Immediately Heather started singing "The Prayer" along with Celine Dion. As Mrs. Murk recognized Heather's voice, she knew that one of her prayers had been answered. This was the second of many more miracles to come.

Just six months before the accident, Heather had been a competitive gymnast. She knew that her top physical shape would help her walk again. But there were so many things that she routinely did without thinking that she now had to learn again. She even had to relearn how to swallow.

Heather put her fierce determination to work, especially motivated by wanting to see her dad. Reading Philippians 1:21-24, "For to me, to live is Christ and to die is gain . . ." (*NIV*), greatly encouraged Heather as she healed. Remembering that God had a purpose and a plan for her life gave her renewed strength during the times when she wanted to just die and go home to Jesus.

A week after the accident, hospital staff could lift Heather into a wheelchair and hold her head. She convinced them to wheel her down the hallway to see her dad. As the aide pushed Heather into her dad's room, Heather's eyes met her dad's eyes for the first time since the accident. She was so thankful that they had both survived, but looking at her dad in traction, Heather knew there were no guarantees of their future or their singing ministry. Gently reaching out to touch her dad, they wept and promised each other that if they ever were able to get back into ministry again, they would record a CD commemorating everything God had done for them. They somehow felt the arms of God wrapping them in His love.

Because of Heather's open wounds, she was prematurely released from the hospital in an effort to protect her from a staph infection that was spreading around the small community hospital.

As Christmas approached, the joy of its celebration took on an entirely different meaning. This year, it was about celebrating life and the One who gives life. The young driver of the 18-wheel gravel truck that hit their van hadn't even seen the construction worker signaling for him to stop. The skid marks showed that he didn't slam on the brakes until two feet before impact. They had no doubt that angels held the truck back from totally crushing them. They were alive for a reason.

The Murk family had a tradition on Christmas morning that Brienne and Heather would sit on the stairs of the house wearing their PJs. Then their parents would tease them about their presents before they could rush to open their gifts. With their dad in the hospital, it just wasn't the same.

On this Christmas morning, Heather, Brienne and Mrs. Murk were all still wearing their green-and-blue plaid PJs when they decided to head over to the hospital and bring Christmas to their dad.

At the hospital, Brienne and her mom pushed Heather in her wheelchair holding the presents on her lap. They also brought eggnog and snacks for the nurses and staff. They had already decorated their dad's traction with flashing Christmas tree lights. Heather hugged her dad, recognizing how fortunate they were to be able to celebrate Christ's birth with the rest of their family.

Both Heather and her dad still had a long road to recovery. Bill remained in the hospital until April. Heather had daily therapy and was forced to use a wheelchair on and off for a few years. The doctors prepared her for the fact that even with massive plastic surgery, her face would never be the face she had before the accident. People actually stopped and stared at her face in disgust. Children were frightened by her scars and would point at her. The Murk family received more than 7,000 cards from around the world after Moody Bible Institute's radio broadcast and other ministries had requested prayer for their family.

One woman came to the hospital after listening to Moody's prayer request for the Murk family and explained that she felt the Lord wanted her to encourage Jeanine about her daughter. "Jeanine, God wants you to know that there will be a day again when Heather will be stopped on the streets because of her beauty," the lady said.

Eventually, Heather had microdermabrasion on her face to remove the top layers of her scar tissue to allow her skin to regrow. Without any other cosmetic surgery, God slowly healed her face, although she continues to pull slivers of glass from her face to this day. Heather shared with me how excited she was when someone recently approached her on the street and told her she was beautiful. That was a timely reminder to her of God's absolute faithfulness in keeping His promises.

Amazingly, barely five months after the accident, the Murks began singing and traveling together again, with Bill performing from a wheelchair.

Three years after the accident that turned their world upside-down, Heather and her dad released their CD entitled *Closer*. Their family still travels and sings together as the group *Myrrh* (www.myrrh.org). Since the name change, in the spring of 2002, hundreds have commented on how they have felt bathed in a sweet-smelling fragrance as they listened to the music and testimony, and were drawn into the presence of the King. As the Murks continue to sing and minister as a family, it's their goal to know God and to make Him known.

Through it all, Heather definitely learned the truth of James 1:2-4 in her classroom of trials. She learned the value of pure joy and the by-product of perseverance. Now a student at Moody Bible Institute, Heather says, "Through our accident, I learned that the joy of the Lord isn't a feeling, but the knowledge that God is in control even when you are facing disappointments or life and death circumstances."

My *Fearful* Child,

Through Jesus, you've gained ACCESS

to the *grace* by which you stand.

Rejoice in the *hope* of My glory. I've given you

a *treasure* in your earthly vessel so that

you rely on My POWER, not your own.

I'll be *magnified* in you whether you live or die.

Life holds many OPPORTUNITIES,

but death also offers eternal gain. Know that

I hear your *desires,* listen to your *cries* and

encourage you. Remember, the path

of the righteous is like the first gleam of dawn.

You'll shine more brilliantly.

Lifting You Up,

YOUR FATHER *of* LIFE

(Romans 5:2; 2 Corinthians 4:7; Philippians 1:20-21; Psalm 10:17; Proverbs 4:18)

83

HEAVENLY FATHER,

I confess that I don't always equate my current trials as joyful gifts. Remind me that there are no accidents with You. Thank You that You're always Sovereign. Thank You for Your promise that You won't abandon me or destroy me. Father, I don't want to quit when I face trouble or obstacles. Help me persevere in:

_____.

Thanks for enduring the pain of the Cross with joy for my sake. Remind me that Your choices are higher than mine. Help me live passionately for You, no matter what I'm doing. I'm looking to You for divine wisdom. It's my goal to be mature and complete. I don't want to be lacking in any area. Please help me focus my passions on the things that will really matter for all eternity.

My *Giving* Child,

Cheerful, unreluctant and noncompulsory

giving refreshes My heart!

Give, and watch Me *give back abundantly.*

Test Me! Watch Me open up

the floodgates of heaven and pour out

overflowing blessings to you in return.

Enriching You,

YOUR HEAVENLY FATHER

(2 Corinthians 9:7; Luke 6:38; Malachi 3:10)

The Best
christmas ever

THE FRESH FRAGRANCE of the scrawny pine tree filled their modest home on the outskirts of Savannah, Georgia. It didn't seem like the typical Christmas. In fact, the temperature was so mild that Charlotte's mama gathered up the pine branches she had placed around the house for decorating and sprayed the tips with silver paint to make them look like they were wearing icicles and snow.

For months, Charlotte's parents had prepared her and her three younger siblings not to expect a big Christmas. Times were especially tough for most families during the Great Depression. But the children were told that they could each count on getting one big gift and a few other small toys from the dime store.

Charlotte never wavered on the one gift she wanted. She had picked out her doll months earlier, and her mama promised that it would be under the tree on Christmas morning. Charlotte even chose the name Jeanie for her cherished doll-to-be.

A wagon train just like the ones in the old Wild West stories pulled into town just blocks away, and Charlotte eagerly ran off to explore. She quickly befriended a barefoot skinny little girl from one of the wagons. The girl's hand-me-down clothes were almost threadbare in places. Charlotte, an inquisitive nine-year-old, was fascinated by the adventurous stories her new friend shared when prompted by Charlotte's barrage of questions as they played together.

"I'm getting my favorite doll for Christmas. What did you ask Santa to bring you?" Charlotte asked her new friend.

"It costs too much to travel all the time, so we don't get presents," the girl replied.

"Where do you put your Christmas tree in your wagon?" Charlotte asked.

"We can't afford a tree either." The little girl whispered these words, showing disappointment in her eyes.

Not wanting to make her playmate sad, Charlotte changed the topic and asked her new friend about happier things in her life.

After hours of playing, Charlotte ran home to retell the adventuresome stories to her mother and siblings.

"Mama, my new friend doesn't get Christmas presents because she's too poor. And they don't even have a Christmas tree," Charlotte said in disbelief.

"Darling, people who live in wagons are called gypsies, and they don't celebrate Christmas," her mama instructed.

"I've always dreamed of traveling around the country," Charlotte said. "But I sure would miss not having Christmas."

The next few days before Christmas, Charlotte enjoyed hearing more adventures from her gypsy friend. Charlotte's mama made cookies for them to share at a tea party. On Christmas Eve, Charlotte fell asleep anticipating finally holding Jeanie the next day. But she also thought about her gypsy friend who wouldn't get any presents and had never owned a doll of her own.

Early Christmas morning, just as promised, Charlotte found Jeanie waiting under the tree. Ripping open the paper, she couldn't believe Jeanie was finally hers. She gave her a big hug and kiss. Charlotte especially loved the pretty blue dress Jeanie wore. It seemed even bluer than she remembered, and blue was Charlotte's favorite color.

She ran to the wagon train to introduce Jeanie to her gypsy friend.

"Wow! I've seen a lot of dolls, but this is by far the prettiest doll I've ever seen. She's so big! You're so lucky to get presents. Maybe one day I'll get a present too," the gypsy girl said longingly. They took turns holding Jeanie, feeding her, dressing her up and rocking her to sleep.

When Charlotte went home, she couldn't stop thinking of her new friend.

"How's Jeanie?" Charlotte's mama asked after she returned from playing at the gypsy camp.

"Jeanie's even better than my dreams, Mama. This is the best Christmas ever. We had so much fun playing with her." Charlotte paused for a minute, then said more softly. "But, Mama, I think God wants me to give Jeanie to my new friend."

"Darling, I'm so proud that you want to share. But I know you, and I know that you'd regret giving your doll away. You've wanted her for so long. And money is so tight that your dad and I couldn't afford to replace Jeanie when you wake up crying in the morning."

Charlotte didn't back down. "Mama, I promise I won't cry in the morning, or ever. I really want to give her Jeanie."

"Let's sleep on it, darling. I know you'll change your mind in the morning," her mama said, kissing her goodnight.

In the morning, when Charlotte still insisted on giving the doll away, her mama finally agreed to let Charlotte give Jeanie to the girl who had nothing. Inspired by Charlotte's generosity, her brother and sisters added some small toys for the other children. They didn't have much, but they collected some clothes they didn't wear anymore. Her mother shared part of their Christmas dinner. And they grabbed some of the silvered pine branches to build a makeshift Christmas tree.

When the whole family arrived at the wagon, the gypsy girl smiled to see Charlotte again.

Charlotte said, "I've been thinking, and I know that Jeanie has always wanted to travel. So I want her to travel with you!"

The skinny gypsy girl must have thought someone would accuse her of stealing. Puzzled, she kept repeating, "For me? For me? For me? You are really giving Jeanie to me?"

Charlotte would never forget seeing the huge smile flash across the gypsy girl's face when she realized that Jeanie was really hers to keep. Visibly overjoyed, she gave Charlotte a gripping hug. The rest of the gypsy family eagerly opened their gifts and dug into the Christmas food in a way that you knew they were really hungry and appreciative.

Charlotte's mama was so surprised the next morning when there were no tears of regret over the generous gift. She knew then that her nine-year-old daughter had learned a precious truth.

Even though Jeanie was Charlotte's last doll, she never regretted giving the doll away. The smile of gratitude on the gypsy girl's face was priceless. The next Christmas, Charlotte started requesting books. More than 50 years later, my friend Charlotte Hale recounts that 1937 was still her favorite Christmas, even though it was definitely her poorest one. She'll never forget the joy of giving away her most desired possession during the ravages of the Great Depression. As an unexpected bonus, she never anticipated that her growing love of reading would lead her to become a bestselling author.

My *Treasured* Child,

I sent Jesus to guarantee you *abundant life*

regardless of your economic condition!

Christmas and life aren't just *about you.*

Love is the greatest and most

unselfish gift you can ever give.

It's important to think about the *needs*

of people. Take advantage of the opportunities

you have to *do good.* I'll make you increase

and abound in love for others.

I'll *bless you* and keep you and make

My face shine upon you. Experience

My *peace* today and always.

Graciously,

YOUR GOD *of* LOVE

(John 10:10; 1 Corinthians 13:5,7; Ephesians 5:16; Numbers 6:24-26)

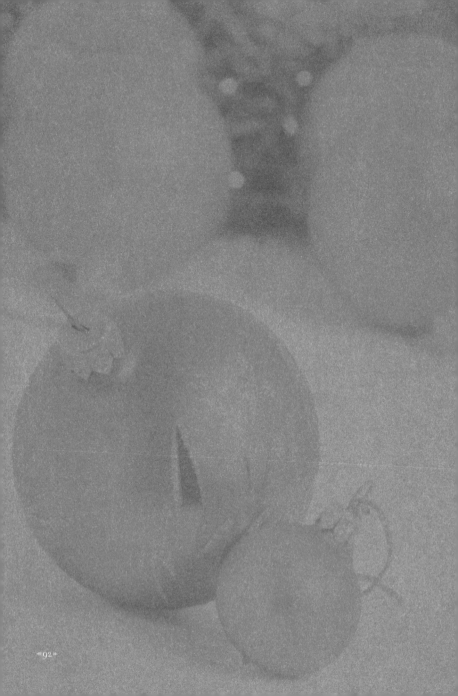

HEAVENLY FATHER,

*Watching TV commercials, it's so easy to get
caught up in the "Give me" materialism of modern
Christmas, focusing on my needs and wants. Forgive
me for my selfishness. Remind me that Christmas is
about celebrating Jesus' birth and love. Thanks that
You loved Me enough to sacrifice Your only Son.
Just as You've loved me unconditionally, help me love
others without any strings attached. Open my eyes to
opportunities to show others Your love by meeting
tangible needs in their lives. Give me a love for others
that goes far beyond the Christmas season. Let love
characterize my daily life so that others will know
that I belong to You! Teach me that it really is more
blessed to give than to receive.*

My *Anguished* Child,

In this world, you can *expect trouble.*

But you can also *take heart,*

knowing that I've already overcome

for you. Your flesh and your heart *may fail,*

but always remember that I am the

Strength *of your heart* and your

Gift forever.

I'll *purify your heart* and renew

a *steadfast spirit* within you.

Changing Your Heart,

YOUR 100-PERCENT FAITHFUL HEAVENLY FATHER

(John 16:33; Psalm 73:26; Psalm 51:10)

Let God's promises shine on your problems.

—CORRIE TEN BOOM

A Heartfelt christmas

"MOMMY, WHEN DO I get to hold him?" Kris's four-year old son, Allan, impatiently asked. He tenderly patted his mother's big tummy. He didn't understand why it was taking so long for his new brother to arrive. His sister, JeriKris, was only a year younger than him, so he really didn't get to be a big brother when she was born. Allan couldn't wait to be a big brother now.

Both of Kris's children were born early. So when her due date of November 28 passed without fanfare, she began to wonder if the little one bulging from inside of her would ever make his grand entrance. She was more than ready for him to come.

December 4, before the sun came up, the long-awaited newest Langston finally entered the world. The nurses cleaned him up and handed Kris and Mike their newest son, reporting that he was a healthy 8 pound, 12 ounce baby.

"Who do you think he looks like?" Mike asked Kris as they studied their newborn's features.

"Are you sure he's our son? He's way too quiet to be a Langston!" Kris commented to Mike. They simultaneously laughed in agreement. The Langston house was always filled with plenty of human energy.

When the pediatrician came to check on little Michael, he reported that everything looked good, although their baby was slightly more blue than he'd prefer. Even that didn't initially raise an alarm.

So when the nurses urgently woke Kris at 3:30 the next morning, she was startled when the doctors came in and told her that her newborn had almost died and was being transferred to a critical care unit at The Arnold Palmer Hospital for Women and Children in Orlando, Florida.

She quickly picked up the phone and called home to wake her husband. "Mike, something is wrong with Michael's heart. He turned blue. But they've stabilized him and are moving him to Arnold Palmer. Please come quickly!"

The next hours were a blur. Mike called Jack, one of the staff pastors at his church. Jack met Mike at the hospital. After talking to Kris, Mike and Jack followed the ambulance to The Arnold Palmer Hospital, while Kris waited to be discharged.

As she waited for the doctors to sign her release papers, Kris fervently prayed for her baby's protection and life. As she did, God impressed on her heart that this was a scenario like the one Abraham faced with his son Isaac, as recorded in the book of Genesis. Kris felt like God was calling her to surrender her newborn to His open arms. She needed to trust that He was in control. "Heavenly Father, if You give us the opportunity to raise Michael David, we'll raise him for You," she promised God.

When Kris finally joined Mike and Jack at the children's hospital, the doctors were catheterizing Michael's heart. It was gut-wrenching to see all the wire and tubes covering his tiny body. Finally, the grim diagnosis came. A team of doctors explained that Michael had a transposed heart. Basically, the two great vessels coming into the heart were in the wrong place, pumping the dirty blood into the body instead of cleaning the blood.

Even their children's hospital wasn't adequately equipped to conduct the needed surgery. They recommended a specialized hospital in Boston, but they were also warned that Michael might not be accepted because he only had one coronary artery to his heart, which would further complicate the surgery.

Kris and Mike had prepared Allan and JeriKris that their baby brother was very ill. But when Mommy and Daddy came home without a baby in their arms, the children didn't understand. "When do I get to hold my brother?" Allan repeatedly asked, trying to grasp where their baby had disappeared.

As they anxiously waited to hear if Boston would perform the surgery, Kris clung to the words of a new song she had learned in church, "Change My Heart, O God." Each time things looked bad, she repeated the words of the song in her heart and felt her faith soar. The words became her constant prayer throughout the ordeal. That became their theme song for Michael. Kris had made a tape of the song to play at the hospital whenever they were gone. Friends from their church joined together to cover the Langston family in prayer.

After what seemed like an eternity, the call came in from Boston that Michael had been accepted into the program. That set off a flurry of motion, coordinating with the hospital and the insurance company, and making travel plans. Kris was disappointed to learn that they couldn't fly on the air ambulance with their baby.

Not wanting her son to be all alone for more than the flight time, Kris prayed that she'd get a commercial flight that would arrive about the same time as the air ambulance. But the earliest flight they could book was scheduled to land in Boston hours after the air ambulance.

Kris knew that God was working behind the scenes when they received a call just before they left for the airport notifying them that the air ambulance's departure had been delayed. In fact, Kris and Mike's plane touched down just minutes after Michael landed in Boston. They had not missed anything significant before they arrived at Children's Hospital Boston.

As the surgeon, Dr. Jonas, spoke to Kris and Mike, they kept their eyes focused on his hands. Knowing that their baby's life depended on this man's hands, they wanted to make sure he had steady hands before they gave him permission to put their precious Michael under the knife. After explaining the procedure, he said he wanted them to observe someone else's baby that had gone through the surgery first. "You need to be prepared for what's coming. It's pretty dramatic," the surgeon warned them.

Mike's face turned white as a ghost when they witnessed another tiny baby in critical care that had been through the same surgery five days earlier. Kris shook her head in horror at the myriad tubes and wires that almost obscured the limp body, realizing that her son would be in that same place in a few days. They felt so helpless. All they could do was lean totally on God.

Kris's parents came to help. And another answer to prayer came when Nancy, a friend from church, was able to fly in to help care for their other two small children. Kris didn't want to leave them at home in Orlando. They couldn't afford to stay at the hotel by the hospital. But Kris and Mike knew they experienced God's favor when they were accepted into a special hospitality program. Their hosts, Dr. and Mrs. Hoppin, offered the Langstons their entire basement so that they could all stay together.

On December 13, Kris decided that she wasn't going to hold Michael before he went into surgery. She was too afraid that he might die during surgery and thought it would be easier not to hold him one last time.

But when the Langstons met the doctors, one of the doctors handed Michael to Kris. That turned out to be a key moment. When Kris held her precious baby, she gained a peace in her heart that she was going to be okay whether Michael lived or died. It was a moment of total surrender to God.

Kris knew she couldn't just sit in the waiting room for up to six grueling hours, with all of those other gravely anxious parents. Instead, her parents volunteered to stay at the hospital while she and Mike took Allan and JeriKris outside to play and make angels in the snow.

When the pager beeped only four hours later, they sensed that it was a good sign that the surgery concluded earlier than expected. Even though they had been prepared, it was still the most difficult thing they have ever experienced to witness all of those tubes and wires camouflaging their baby. But when Kris saw signs that Michael's kidneys were working and noticed that the doctors were able to enclose his incision, she rested a bit easier that night. They were relieved when Michael's condition was upgraded several times to a lower level of critical care over the next days.

Michael's condition improved so quickly that Kris and Mike couldn't believe it when they were released to go home early. When they brought him home, he was 7 pounds, 13 ounces. They were a bit nervous as the hospital handed them their still frail baby to fly home. They arrived home just four days before Christmas. Friends from church came by to show their love. Kris's eyes teared up when she opened the packaged ornament her friend Gail handmade for her. The ornament said, "Change My Heart, O God. December 1992."

This true story is especially close to my heart, because I witnessed much of it firsthand. Kris and Mike Langston were the singles' leaders at my church when I was in college. I spent many nights hanging out with them. It was exciting to see the transformation that occurred in Kris's life as she allowed God to change her spiritual heart to make her more like Him through this trial.

I'll never forget what Kris shared with us that Christmas after almost losing her son. She had a new appreciation of what Christmas was all about. She reflected how Michael's near-death showed them the enormity of what God sacrificed by giving up His only Son, knowing that He would die on the cross 33 years later.

Today Michael is a healthy teenager. Recently, at his annual heart check-up, his doctor told Michael that he couldn't believe Michael had been a transposition heart baby. He predicts that Michael will be over

6' 4" by the time he finishes growing. Usually, children who have experienced his condition are frail. Michael told me that he knows that God gave him the gift of life for a special purpose. He believes that God may be calling him into youth ministry.

Trials teach us what we are; they dig up the soil,
and let us see what we are made of.

—CHARLES HADDON SPURGEON

My *Drained* Child,

Above all, *guard your heart,*

for it is the wellspring of your life.

Be strong and take heart when you

hope in Me. *Don't be afraid* or

overwhelmed. Remember that

I'm your God. I will strengthen

you and uphold you with My right hand.

I'll give you an *undivided heart*

and energize you with

My *renewing spirit.*

I'll remove your calloused heart and

replace it with a heart that's tender.

Making You More Like Me,

YOUR GOD

(Proverbs 4:23; Psalm 31:24; Isaiah 41:10; Ezekiel 11:19)

My *Troubled* Child,

I've created today for *joy* and *gladness*.

Focus on *true and noble things.*

Think about everything that is *right,*

pure and *sweet*. Reflect on whatever is

admirable, excellent or *praiseworthy*.

Remember that the ability to enjoy your life

and work, and to *accept your role in life,*

is a gift from Me.

Joyfully,

YOUR CREATOR

(Psalm 118:24; Philippians 4:8; Ecclesiastes 5:19-20)

when Family must
Be apart

NIKKI AND JEREMY'S FIRST CHILD, Harper, was born on December 3, 2007. Nikki's parents had driven up to Charleston from Atlanta after they received the 3 A.M. wake-up call that Nikki's water had broken. Jeremy's mom drove up from Birmingham; his dad followed shortly after his grandson was born. Weighing in at a whopping 9 pounds, 12 ounces, the doctor delivered Harper a week early by C-section because of his size. Nikki didn't mind Harper's early arrival, because she knew her husband's days of bonding with their newborn were numbered.

Jeremy is a C-17 pilot in the Air Force, so Nikki was grateful that he was able to be there for the birth of their son. She knew of so many other military wives who had delivered their babies without their husbands to coach and support them through a delivery.

But this special time of celebration was also bittersweet because Jeremy's squadron was being deployed just four days after Christmas. Nikki was so proud of her husband for serving his country. But she also knew the personal sacrifice his service would cost their growing family. Jeremy would probably miss many of Harper's important developmental milestones. Nikki wondered,

Will Jeremy be there the first time Harper rolls over? Will he see Harper sit up? Will he be here the first time Harper crawls? Will he miss Harper's first words or first steps? How many Christmases will we be separated in the future? She had always known there were no guarantees, but still it was difficult to think of his absence, especially now. With Jeremy overseas, she would virtually be a single mom at times.

Instead of focusing on their imminent separation, Nikki and Jeremy made a choice to savor every moment together as a family their first Christmas. They bought a huge Christmas stocking and had Harper's name embroidered on it. Then they placed their son in the stocking and posed him for adorable pictures. Next they placed Harper under the tree as if he were their present to each other, and took more pictures. There was no doubt that Harper was God's best Christmas present to them ever, with the exception of the gift of Jesus. There were a lot of other "Kodak moments" during the next weeks. When Santa came around their base housing on a red fire engine, they grabbed the baby and the camera and rushed outside for a picture.

They made a special effort to establish some family traditions that mirrored their values. They prioritized participating in church because they wanted their baby to know from his very first Christmas the real meaning of the season. Wanting to plant seeds of faith in his life as early as they could, they took turns reading the Christmas story to their baby.

Jeremy invested as much time as he could to get to know his son. He even volunteered to change diapers in the middle of the night, realizing that he wouldn't be able to hold Harper much longer.

On Christmas Day, Nikki and Jeremy focused on the gift of just being together, trying hard not to think about Jeremy's leaving for South East Asia. There were a lot of tears on December 29, as they headed for the Air Force base. Jeremy's squadron had a gathering for all the families at the terminal at Charleston Air Force Base an hour before they were scheduled to fly out. All the men and women looked so sharp in their desert-colored flight uniforms. The Red Cross provided coffee and doughnuts. Hugs, kisses, and tears were in abundance before Jeremy filed in line behind his fellow pilots headed down the hallway to board their plane.

After the farewell, and later that afternoon at home, the doorbell rang announcing a flower delivery. Jeremy had sent Nikki a big colorful bouquet of daisies, lilies and mixed flowers. Nikki cried as she read the sweet note accompanying the flowers: "I miss you already. Take care of Harper for me. I love you. See you soon. Love, Jeremy."

Nikki thought of Numbers 6:24-26, the Scripture passage that God had used to encourage her as she prepared for Jeremy's overseas deployment. She began praying it: "Heavenly Father, bless Jeremy and keep him safe. Make Your face shine upon him and be gracious to him. Turn Your face toward him and give him peace. And please keep him safe until he comes back home to Harper and me."

She knew that God understood the sacrifice and heartache of separation and loneliness she was now experiencing. After all, that is the true miracle of Christmas—that God sent His Son Jesus to Earth so that we could receive His ultimate gift of adoption as His sons and daughters.

Joy is the echo of God's life in us.

—JOSEPH MARMION

My *Chosen* Child,

Remember, My Name is your Strong Tower.
When you run to Me, you'll find safety.
In Christ, I've given you *every* spiritual blessing
in the heavenly world. Even before
I created the world, I *chose you*.
Through Jesus, I redeemed you and prepared
a way for you to be *adopted* as My child.
I've *freely given* you gifts of glorious grace,
wisdom and understanding. I always watch
over you, without sleeping. There is *never*
a moment when My eye is not on you.
You can trust Me to faithfully *guard*
your comings and goings wherever you are.

Abundantly Blessing You,

YOUR LORD *and* HEAVENLY FATHER

(Proverbs 18:10; Ephesians 1:3-9; Psalm 121:3-8)

GRACIOUS HEAVENLY FATHER,

It's so easy to lose the joy of today by worrying about what

may or may not happen tomorrow. Don't let me lose sight of

that. Help me see each day as a gift from You. Give me Your

perspective. I need wisdom. Teach me to number my days.

Fill me with Your joy, which isn't reliant on my circumstances.

Help me be an ambassador of Your joy. Let others see a

difference in me that is only explainable in terms of who

You are. Thanks for being the lifter of my countenance.

You have made me glad, and I rejoice in You!

Keeping Christ in Christmas

- Invite a local serviceman to share your family's Thanksgiving or Christmas dinner.

- Offer to baby-sit for the spouse of a deployed military person so that she (or he) can shop for Christmas or just relax and refresh for a few hours.

- Offer to bring meals to the family of someone serving in the military.

- Place a wreath on the tombstone of a military hero who has paid the ultimate sacrifice for our freedom.

- Remember a serviceman's family during Christmas when finances are probably tight. Bring gifts for the children. Gift certificates for restaurants would bless the spouse. Let the family know how much you appreciate their sacrifice as their loved one defends our country.

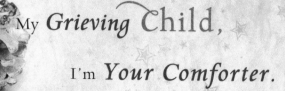

My *Grieving* Child,

I'm *Your Comforter.*

Your tears aren't wasted. When you

sow in tears, you'll reap with *songs of joy.*

Please don't *settle* for mere survival . . . I sent

Jesus to give you *abundant life!*

I keep your *lamp burning* and turn your

darkness into light.

Wiping Your Tears Away,

YOUR GOD *of* ALL COMFORT

(Isaiah 51:12; Psalm 126:5; John 10:10; Psalm 18:28)

The christmas star

ONE OF MY DEAR and most joyful friends, Susan Duke, has the gift of Christmas cheer all year round. You can just see the joy of Jesus all over her countenance. Whenever we get together, our visits are filled with lots of laughter. She's truly learned how to embrace life with passion. Susan is a former antiques dealer and is known for decorating her house to the hilt for Christmas. To me, she's like a kinder, gentler version of Martha Stewart. Groups have even requested to pay to hold Christmas parties at her home in Greenville, Texas. That's why I was so surprised when Susan first shared her testimony to me about the Christmas she didn't want to celebrate.

It was December 1990. Susan sat on her living room floor in front of boxes of Christmas decorations. Usually, Susan loved trips down nostalgia lane as she unpacked the boxes, thinking about the significance of the special ornaments and keepsake memories of past Christmases with her family. But this year, she wept thinking of the memories contained in those boxes. Just eight weeks earlier, Susan and Harvey's 18-year-old son, Thomas, had been killed in a car accident. Their older daughter, Kelly, was already married and a mom herself, living several hours away. So Susan was suddenly faced with an empty nest for the first time at Christmas.

Ever since Thomas was a small child, Christmas had been his favorite time of the year. Over the years, he had faithfully saved his allowance money to buy very thoughtful gifts for his family and friends. His generous nature always touched his mother's heart.

Tears streamed down Susan's cheeks. She wondered, *How can the world go on celebrating Christmas as if nothing has happened? It just doesn't seem fair.* Susan wanted to cancel Christmas this year. *After all, how could their family celebrate without Thomas?* But their church youth group had made a special request to have a celebration of Thomas's life at the Duke house. Susan knew that Thomas's friends were grieving too.

His friends had volunteered to decorate the tree for Susan at their Christmas get-together. This year, Susan struggled just to put up the bare tree and a few other decorations. It had been such an emotionally draining day that she fell asleep almost as soon as she lay down on her bed that night. In a deep sleep, she began to dream.

In her dream, Susan and Harvey were standing outside, gazing at the brilliant night sky. They stood arm in arm, breathing the crisp night air as they looked up at millions of shimmering stars. Susan tearfully told her husband, "Christmas will never be the same without Thomas. We'll never be able to give Thomas another gift, and he'll never be able to give us the gifts he so loved to give at Christmas."

As they stood watching the starry sky, Susan's attention was drawn to one particularly large star just to the left of the multitude of other stars. All of a sudden that bright star rapidly shot across the sky, moving to the right. But then it curved and zoomed right toward them just over their heads. When the star disappeared, Susan clearly heard the voice she loved so well say, "Mom, that star was for you."

Susan turned toward Harvey and said, "Did you hear that? Did you hear Thomas's voice? He just sent me a star! What a gift!" And then her dream ended.

The next morning, when Susan awoke, she still felt a new sense of peace, thanks to the unmistakable voice of her son in her dream. That dream had touched her spiritually, emotionally and physically. She had renewed strength for the next few days of preparation for the party in honor of Thomas.

Susan placed a small tree decorated with angels in Thomas's old bedroom window. That was the first time she realized that she could do something special to remember and honor her son.

She wondered if she was placing too much emphasis on her dream. But her thoughts about the dream kept lingering and she couldn't ignore the unexplainable peace it gave her aching heart as she continued to clean and prepare for the next few days.

The evening of the tribute to Thomas, Susan and Harvey greeted each teen with a hug. Laughter and joy filled their house for the first time in weeks as Thomas's friends decorated the tree and imparted life to the Dukes' grief-stricken hearts. Their tender expressions of love gave Susan a glimpse of hope that her empty arms would be able to embrace life once again one day.

The party started winding down around midnight. Susan took their dog, Bo, outside. It was a brisk cold night. She looked up and noticed the endless stars. That's when she realized the sky looked just like her dream.

Waiting for Bo to come to the porch, Susan closed her eyes and whispered, "Thomas, I'm waiting for my star."

Bo came back to go inside and Susan got distracted washing dishes. She could hear some of the teenagers going outside. About 10 minutes passed before a loud commotion. One of the teenage girls ran into the kitchen and beckoned, "Hurry! Come to the backyard! Hurry and come with me before it's gone!"

Susan dropped her dishcloth and took the teen's hand. "Before *what's* gone?" "The star," the girl said, as they walked outside. The teen was disappointed when she couldn't locate what she wanted to show Thomas's mom.

As Susan asked for an explanation, another teen jumped into the conversation.

"You just won't believe what we saw! As we were standing around talking about how bright the stars are tonight, we spotted one star that was far brighter than the others. It hung perfectly still for a long time. Then suddenly it took off and shot across the sky." They all shared that it wasn't an ordinary shooting star. The light had filled the yard so intensely that one of the girls became frightened. She fell to her knees and started praying.

Susan shared with Thomas's friend Heather that she had just told Thomas she was waiting for her star. Susan had no doubt the star was a gift from Thomas.

"Let's go inside and gather around the fireplace, and I'll share about my dream a few nights ago," Susan said, beckoning to the remaining teens.

They all sat around the fireplace as Susan recounted her earlier dream. She knew they had been given a message far greater than just a dream about a special star. They talked about the first Christmas and the star that led the way to the baby in the manger. It was an incredible time of sharing their thoughts about grief, life longings and what really matters in life. They cried together, laughed together and embraced each other. One of the teens even rededicated his life to God.

By the time the gathering ended, everyone had been deeply impacted. After seeing the last of the teens out, Susan stayed on the porch reflecting on the entire night. She looked up at the stars and prayed, "Thank You, God, for Bethlehem's star. And thank You for sending me some earthly angels tonight— to share Thomas's gift."

Susan never forgot that Christmas and how God filled her grieving soul with gratitude, wonder and certainty that, over time, He would mend her broken heart.

To Susan, the star represented love that never dies. She realized that because Christ came, love never has to say good-bye.

Stars became symbolic in their family's healing. Susan's daughter, Kelly, also experienced tremendous grief over her brother. That first Christmas, Susan and Kelly exchanged one gift labeled "From Thomas." That started their mother-daughter tradition of exchanging stars, symbolizing the hope and promise that they would see their beloved Thomas again in heaven one day. But the inspiring story of hope doesn't end there.

When Susan started speaking, she often retold her star story when she was asked to share her testimony. Each time she shared this story, several people came up to her and asked if she had written the story down so that they could share it with others. She always said, "No, but one day I will write it."

In July 1996, she finally typed her story and submitted it to *HomeLife* magazine. Before she sealed the envelope, she thought of changing the title. She really wanted to call it "A Gift from Thomas." But fearing that the editor would prefer a simpler title, she simply called it "The Star."

After she mailed her story, she learned that she had already missed the deadline for the Christmas issue. So the next month, she was pleasantly surprised when she received a contract in the mail for her star story.

On November 8, Susan picked up a package from *Home Life* magazine from the post office. When she returned home, she opened the package and pulled out three complimentary copies of *HomeLife* magazine. Inside the cover of the magazine was the first story she'd ever written or submitted to a publisher.

Susan took a deep breath, turned the page, and there, spread across a layout of a beautiful midnight blue sky, was the title in bold white print: "A Gift from Thomas." Tears of surprised joy streamed down her cheeks as she realized the editor had discarded her make-do title and given her tribute the exact title she had envisioned. And she couldn't help but wonder, *Is it just a coincidence that this magazine has arrived today—November 8—on Thomas's birthday?*

Susan didn't hear an audible voice, but she knew that if Thomas could tell her in person, he'd say, "See, Mom, the star I sent you wasn't just a gift for you, but also for many others."

Little did she realize that her first published article would start her down a path of writing inspirational books. One of her many books, *Grieving Forward: Embracing Life Beyond Loss*, which she wrote in 2006, is especially near to her heart as it candidly details her long journey from the valley of the shadow of death to rediscovering a life of purpose and incredible joy. Susan's life is an example that hope is alive, and that healing will triumph.

May you be wise and shine like the brightness of the heavens.
May you lead many to righteousness, like the stars forever and ever.

— DANIEL 12:3

My *Saddened* Child,

I shine on those living in *darkness* in the shadow of death. I've taken up your infirmities and *carried your sorrows*. I am a refuge for the oppressed, a *stronghold* in times of trouble. I am the *Resurrection* and the Life. Anyone who *believes* in Me will live, even though he dies.... And anyone who lives and believes in Me will never die.

Love,

YOUR GOD *of* EVERLASTING LIFE

(Luke 1:79; Isaiah 53:4; Psalm 9:9; John 11:25-26)

DEAR FATHER,

I confess that I'm at a point in my life where I don't feel like celebrating. Right now my world looks pretty dark and bleak. I'm tired of crying. I am frazzled and struggling to even take a step. I need Your light to shine on me.

For those who have lost a loved one, Christmas can be a difficult time of the year, even decades after the loss. In *Grieving Forward*, Susan Duke shares some excellent ideas for coping with loss during Christmas:

- Plan ahead for special occasions and discuss with other family members ways to honor your loved ones, and perhaps start some new traditions.

- Find something symbolic that represents or honors your loved one in a special way.

- One church puts a remembrance tree in its foyer every Christmas adorned with picture-framed ornaments and photos of lost loved ones to help church families remember.

- Make holidays meaningful by reaching out to someone.

- Give the money you would have spent on a loved one to a charity or to someone in need.

- Give flowers to your church, hospital or another organization as a memorial to your loved one.

- Listen to music that will lift your spirits during difficult days or seasons.

- Write a letter to your loved one each year on his or her birthday or at Christmas. Write everything you feel. Keep your letters in a special box or send them one by one heavenward on the end of a helium balloon as a symbolic release.

My *Distressed* Child,

Let your soul rest in Me alone.

I'm your *only Rock* and
your Salvation. I'm your Stronghold.

You'll always find *refuge* in Me.

You can always trust in Me and
pour out your heart to Me at
all times. I'm the Source of all hope.

I'll fill you with all *joy and peace*

as you trust in Me, blessing your life with

hope by the power of My Spirit.

Waiting for You,
YOUR SAFE HAVEN

(Psalm 62:5-8; Romans 15:13)

THE CHARLIE BROWN
TREE OF HOPE

ALTHOUGH THIS IS A TRUE STORY, the names have been changed. David, Lori's husband, served with distinction as a captain in the Air Force. They were stationed in St. Louis, Missouri, but David had traveled to Oklahoma for three months of training. When his commanding officer came to the door that September day of 1973, dressed in an official black suit and accompanied by another officer, Lori knew something was desperately wrong and feared the worst. *Had there been a crash during testing?*

Never in her wildest dreams did she expect to hear that her husband had been jailed after he was found aimlessly wandering around and acting strangely. When the police discovered his identity, they called his commanding officer. Later, David was transferred to Sheppard Air Force Base in Texas for psychological/psychiatric evaluation.

After the officers left, Lori immediately called her mom and sister as she quickly packed her suitcase. They all agreed to rendezvous at the airport to pick up Lori and David's two small children before Lori boarded a flight to Texas.

When Lori saw David for the first time at the hospital in Sheppard Air Force Base, he was heavily sedated and mumbling. He was also locked in a padded room with no furniture. There was only a mattress on the floor. It was a dramatic change from the confident and highly respected husband she had married six years earlier.

Lori couldn't believe the doctors' diagnosis of paranoid schizophrenia. David had never shown any signs of mental problems and had always been the model of responsibility and stability. It was an overnight "extreme makeover" of the worst imaginable kind.

At the hospital, voices inaudible to anyone else taunted David. He reported hearing messages. He'd imagine hearing a partial sentence and build a reality that took him down a treacherous dark path. He didn't even know what was real anymore. Within a few hours, he went from a top leader of military recruiters to someone with shattered confidence. It was almost like he was starring in a bizarre episode of *The Twilight Zone*.

Mystified, Lori asked the doctors what had triggered his psychological problems. Although David had battled a bad case of bronchitis for three weeks, he never experienced any warning signs of any mental irregularities. One moment he was fine. Then he took a break from studying to have a beer with some friends. After leaving the party at his friend's apartment, it was as if his mind just snapped. Suddenly, he felt like he had "super powers" and started hearing tormenting voices in his mind.

David's abrupt personality change stumped the doctors. The only possible explanation they could offer Lori was that David's medication for his bronchitis, mixed with alcohol, somehow triggered his psychotic episodes.

Lori stayed with her husband for a week but had to fly home when her dad underwent emergency lung surgery. It was as if her whole life had collapsed in a few weeks. The doctors didn't give David's prognosis much hope, and warned Lori that her husband would probably never be able to hold a job again. During many sleepless nights, she worried how she would be able to provide for her family. *How would this affect their children's future?* She felt as if she were in a deep, dark pit with no escape.

Both Lori and David had grown up in the church. But after their wedding, in the busyness of everyday life, they had drifted away from their faith. Neither of them had been taught how to have a personal relationship with God or how to study the Bible. The desperation of this crisis sparked both of them to reexamine their faith once again.

As he slowly walked into the hospital chapel, David picked up a tract by Norman Vincent Peale called "Quit Worrying." Under the effects of the medication, his attention span was miniscule. But the tract was written in a narrative fashion that he could comprehend. Reading it over and over helped him discern the unreal. He realized that his bizarre ideas had been dominated by a break from reality. The Air Force chaplain reached out to David. Meanwhile, back home, Lori's mom's pastor was ministering to her fears of an unknown future. He encouraged her with God's promises in the Bible.

As David started meditating on biblical promises by listening to Scripture tapes, the dark voices eventually stopped. As he focused on the truth of God's Word, he learned to listen for God's voice. David's prayer life took on new meaning too. His conversations with God became his lifeline to reality and truth.

After David was transferred out of the mental ward, he still faced a tremendous battle ahead. The medications had long-term side effects. David was extremely frustrated when trying to do common, everyday tasks, and he struggled just to walk. The doctors started cutting his medications so that Lori would be able to take him home. But David's prognosis for recovery still looked bleak.

Needing hope, Lori clung to the promises of Psalm 91. Every day she asked God to keep His wings over David, to protect him and keep him safe from the effects of the medication.

Lori and David flew home just before Thanksgiving time. When they'd go shopping at the BX, David couldn't even manage to make the change to pay. In public, he depended on Lori for everything. He had lost all confidence in his ability, and his self-esteem was at an all-time low. David wondered if he would ever be able to return to "normal." Even talking on the phone was hard for him.

Having been an independent executive all of his life, he felt utterly help-less and struggled with depression over the difficulty of accomplishing the most menial tasks. And Lori was exhausted being a caregiver on top of her responsibilities raising their two- and four-year-old children virtually alone. They both wanted their old lives back.

A few weeks before Christmas, their neighbor, Larry, invited David to come with him to cut down a Christmas tree. At first, David didn't feel up to it. But Lori thought it was a good idea and finally convinced him to try for their son, Tim's, sake. David and Tim joined Larry's family in search of Christmas trees.

Hours later, the doorbell rang. David slowly staggered forward, pulling a small Christmas tree. It was one of the ugliest trees Lori had ever seen. It reminded her of the scrawny branches of the infamous tree in Charlie Brown's Christmas—mostly twigs with sparse patches of evergreen. But it was also one of the most beautiful sights when Lori noticed that tears were run-ning down her husband's face. It was the first time he had done something by himself since September. His tears gave Lori hope for the future. It was a sign that he was finally starting to come home in spirit. It was a special Christmas just being together as a family again.

Cutting down that tree had marked an important landmark in David's progress. He felt that he hadn't let his family down, as he had for so long in the months before that day. Cutting down the tree symbolized the first time David felt that he had actually done something right and useful again. Pleasing his family made him feel so good.

Slowly, he started doing routine tasks again. One day at the BX, he was able to write a check to pay without getting help. David felt another big boost after his mother-in-law commented one day how "confidently he was walking." Eventually, David started regaining his confidence on the phone. Next, he was able to leave the house without his wife. Then he began to take on more responsibility with their children and household tasks. He even was able to return to work part-time.

David and Lori both started to dream again. Before the end of 1974, David was totally off medication and he has never had any mental problems since. It was a total healing that was amazing even to David's doctors. They had considered him disabled for life and had already begun the paperwork to process him out of the military with a medical discharge. Instead, David continued his career, was chosen for special assignments, was promoted twice and given leadership positions of increasing responsibility. Ultimately, he was trusted with the highest security clearances, handling the most sensitive defense information. David went on to become a top corporate leader and a senior political advisor.

Looking back, Lori and David are grateful that God used this trial to bring them back to a personal relationship with Him. Now they enjoy spending time together reading and studying the promises of the Bible and mentoring others in how to have a deep and intimate relationship with their faithful God. And it's given them compassion for families who are faced with a loved one who suffers from mental illness.

I would have despaired unless I had believed that
I would see the goodness of the Lord in the land of the living.
Wait for the Lord; Be strong, and let your heart take courage;
Yes, wait for the Lord.

PSALM 27:13-14 (NASB)

He who has not Christmas in his heart

will never find it under a tree.

−ROY L. SMITH

My *Doubtful* Child,

I haven't given you a *spirit* of fear. Instead I've given you life-changing *power*, *love* and a *sound mind*.

When you feel like your life is slipping, I support you. My consolation brings joy to your soul, relieving your anxiety. Let your soul praise Me. Don't forget My incomparable benefits. There isn't any sin I can't forgive or any disease or addiction that I cannot heal.

I redeem you from the pits of life, blessing you with My *love* and *compassion*. Watch Me satisfy your desires with good things and renew your youth. Let your soul rest again. For I've been good to you.

I've delivered your soul from death, wiped your tears from your eyes and kept your feet from stumbling. I've called you to live!

Supporting You,

YOUR EVERLASTING FATHER

(2 Timothy 1:7; Psalm 94:18-19; Psalm 103:2-5; Psalm 116:7-9)

DEAR LORD,

It's easy to get discouraged and weary with all
the extra expectations and activities of Christmas.
I need You to be my Refuge and my Strength every
day. The world makes a lot of promises that it can
never fulfill, often leading to depression. Forgive me
for searching for hope in all the wrong places.
Help me wait on You and find my hope in You alone.
Whenever I get overwhelmed, help me look up to You
first instead of running to a friend or loved one.
Constantly remind me that You're my Helper.
Help me leave all my worries with You, trusting that
You know what's best and You deeply care for me.
Remind me to reflect upon You in my day-to-day life.
And please make me sensitive to others who are
struggling during the holidays and need encouraging
reminders of the promises of Your Hope. I'm so
grateful that You give us opportunities to experience
and reflect Your goodness on Earth! 🎁

The spirit of christmas

Take a few moments to reflect on the goodness of God and how He has been good to you. Read 2 Corinthians 3:18. Does your face reflect the hope of His goodness? I like this thought from Max Lucado:

> A vibrant shining face is the mark of one who has stood in God's presence. . . . God is in the business of changing the face of the world.[1]

Did you know that Christmas is the highest time for suicides?

We can never untangle all the woes in other people's lives. We can't produce miracles overnight. But we can bring a cup of cool water to a thirsty soul, or a scoop of laughter to a lonely heart.

— BARBARA JOHNSON

1. Max Lucado, *Just Like Jesus* (Nashville, TN: Word Publishing, 1998), p. 83.

My *Busy* Child,

In the midst of the Christmas rush,

come to Me when you are *frazzled*

and ***worn out***. I'll give you REST.

Learn from Me and you won't be overburdened.

I'll show you how to find balance.

Take time to be STILL and *know* that I am your

God! Set your affections on what

really matters . . .

not on the *trivial* pursuits of life that try

to distract you from Me.

Refreshing and Refocusing You,

YOUR GOD *of* PURPOSE

(Matthew 11:28-30; Psalm 46:10; Colossians 3:1-2)

Then the Grinch thought of something he hadn't before. What if Christmas,
he thought, doesn't come from a store. What if Christmas, perhaps, means
a little bit more. – DR. SEUSS, *The Grinch Who Stole Christmas*

the christmas when
LESS MEANT MORE

EVER SINCE MARCIA'S TWO DAUGHTERS were little, the family tradition had been to go overboard with Christmas decorations. She always believed "the more the merrier" when it came to decorations and festivities. Her holidays always revolved around lots of gifts, people and excitement.

November 11, 2007, Marcia's youngest daughter, Rachel, was married after a two-year engagement. It was a blessing to have many of her family fly in to West Palm Beach all the way from Brazil and other parts of the country to celebrate Rachel's marriage. While Marcia was thrilled with her new son-in-law, she wasn't prepared for the sadness that came after the wedding when she experienced a severe case of empty-nest syndrome. She struggled to accept that her child-rearing days were over for good, and she also suffered from emotional burnout and just plain physical exhaustion. She couldn't hold back the tears anymore.

A few weeks later, while driving to her daughter's house for dinner, Marcia said to her husband, "Dana, in the midst of planning for the wedding and catching up at my two offices, I can't believe that I totally forgot that we need to schedule time to get all those boxes out of the attic to start decorating for Christmas."

She sounded so overwhelmed; still, she was shocked to hear Dana say, "Marcia, do you really have to decorate and do it all this year?"

Marcia had never considered that option before. She always did things over the top. Even though she'd been through self-help classes, she still struggled with over-performance issues.

Soon they had reached their daughter's house. Thanksgiving was a joyous family time together, especially having Rachel home from her honeymoon.

Over the next few days, Marcia tried to get caught up at her office while she kept thinking of the daunting task of preparing for Christmas. For some reason, she couldn't put the idea her husband had planted out of her mind—*Do you really have to do it all this year?*

But the more she thought about it, the more she actually considered his suggestion. Marcia reflected on the Serenity Prayer she had learned in her self-help class:

> God grant me the serenity to accept the things
> I cannot change, courage to change the things I can,
> and the wisdom to know the difference.[1]

Now she felt a freedom to share her idea of downsizing Christmas this year with her husband. After all, it was inspired by his question. He was surprised but pleased with Marcia's change of heart.

Next, she talked about her idea with her daughters. Rachel knew that her mother was exhausted from wedding festivities and nodded her agreement. Elizabeth interjected, "Mom, it won't seem like Christmas, but I can see that you need and deserve a break."

Finally it was time to share her decision with other family and friends. Marcia explained that she wasn't going to hold her traditional Christmas this year. She wasn't going to entertain or shop till she dropped, exchange gifts, decorate at all, attend scores of Christmas parties, make her Christmas feast or even send Christmas cards. She didn't want to be the Grinch who stole Christmas, but she did want to spend time with her family and reflect on the true meaning of Christmas—celebrating Christ's birthday. And that's just what she did.

A few weeks before Christmas, she made deposits into her daughters' bank accounts so that they could buy what they really wanted for Christmas.

On Christmas Eve, Marcia enjoyed a relaxing evening with her husband, daughter Elizabeth, and two friends. They had a simple lasagna meal. The only decorations were white candles on the table. And it didn't take hours to clean up the kitchen like it usually did after her traditional Christmas feast. Instead they sat in the living room leisurely talking about life without the typical holiday stresses.

At their Christmas Eve service, the pastor preached about the simplicity in which Jesus came to Earth. That message especially touched Marcia's heart. Instead of feeling her typical holiday stress, Marcia reflected on the good news that Jesus came to us.

On Christmas morning, Marcia and Dana enjoyed sleeping in late and casually talking about the upcoming year while in the comfort of their bed. Then she spent time talking on the phone with family in Brazil. There was none of the usual flurry of Christmases past. That afternoon, they went to Rachel's house for a late lunch. Her daughter cooked an amazing meal. They had fun playing games together, listening to music and looking at wedding pictures. Rachel even exchanged a few gifts with her new mother-in-law.

Then Marcia and Dana went home and just relaxed. Later, she called family and friends and enjoyed sharing with each one how much she uniquely appreciated them.

The next few days, she didn't have to waste time taking down Christmas decorations or standing in those outrageous lines waiting to return or exchange gifts. Instead, she spent more time reading the Bible and praying. With the new year coming, she reflected on Proverbs 31. Usually when she read Proverbs 31, it made her feel like she had to perform to an almost unattainable standard. But this year, verse 25 encouraged her heart:

> *She is clothed with strength and dignity; she can laugh at the days to come.*

Marcia thought about the things in life that she had once feared and now could actually laugh about. She thanked God for the laughter that filled this special Christmas as her family spent extra time together.

New Year's day was pure and good. She started the year refreshed. Looking back, she cherishes the memories from her nontraditional Christmas and is tempted to do it again sometime or at least scale back. She'll never forget the freedom she found when Christmas involved *less* and turned out to be *more* about the things that truly mattered to her.

My *Burned-Out* Child,

Don't try to do life by your own *might*

or *power*. Instead, live by My Spirit.

I'm with you and *mighty* to save.

I take great delight in you, quieting you with My love.

Pray for everyone in authority. Discover a

peaceful and quiet life in all *godliness* and *holiness*.

Restoring You,

YOUR LORD *of* ALL

(Zechariah 4:6; Zephaniah 3:17; 1 Timothy 2:1-3)

keeping christ in christmas

To help you stay focused on the heart of the season, choose a quiet place to set
a nativity scene (even if it's in the bathroom) and find some quiet moments
every day this month to hold the baby Jesus in your hands and know that
He holds you in His.[2]

1. The Serenity Prayer was written by theologian Reinhold Niebuhr in the 1930s for a sermon and is widely
   used by others.

2. Karla Dornacher, *The Heart & Home of Christmas* (Nashville, TN: J Countryman ® division of Thomas
   Nelson Book Group, 2004), p. 25.

My *Very Important* Child,

It's natural to get tired at times.

Just remember, when you wait and
hope in Me, I'll renew your strength

and help you to *thrive* in life.

Don't worry; even when it looks like

everything is falling apart, I'm working

behind the scenes *for you.* I love to do far

beyond all that you can ask or dream,

according to My power,

which is at work *in your life.*

Rest in Me,

YOUR GOD *of* ALL HOPE

(Isaiah 40:30-31; Ephesians 3:19-20)

*The joy of brightening other lives, bearing each others' burdens, easing oth-
ers' loads and supplanting empty hearts and lives with generous gifts becomes
for us the magic of Christmas.* – W . C . J O N E S

Nathaniel's Hope

NEVER IN THEIR WILDEST DREAMS did the Kucks
imagine that one of the most dismal Christmases of their life would
be the catalyst for a vision to encourage and give hope to thousands of
others. Tim and Marie Kuck looked forward to celebrating their son,
Nathaniel's, first Christmas at home with their two young daughters,
Brianna and Ashley.

When Nathaniel Timothy Kuck was born prematurely on
June 6, 1997, Marie almost died delivering him by C-section. Even after
extended genetic testing, Nathaniel's doctors couldn't diagnose his rare
syndrome. During the next three months, Nathaniel needed several surgeries and remained in the Neonatal Intensive Care Unit at Arnold Palmer
Children's Hospital. He came home for the first time on Marie's birthday,
and his health was very fragile for the next few months, with repeated visits
to the hospital with respiratory issues.

Taking care of any infant's needs can be exhausting, but Nathaniel
required grueling around-the-clock care. After spending so much of
their past months at the hospital on an emotional roller coaster, they
were just happy that Nathaniel could be home to celebrate Jesus' birth.

Unexpectedly, on Christmas morning, they had to rush Nathaniel
back to the hospital. Instead of gathering around a towering Christmas
tree piled with gifts and enjoying a special family time, the Kucks spent
the whole day at the hospital huddled around Nathaniel's crib, feeling all
alone and robbed of any Christmas joy.

Later that afternoon, Tim and Marie headed for the cafeteria, anticipating a much-needed lunch break with their daughters. Much to their disappointment, even the hospital cafeteria was closed for the holiday. So their Christmas "dinner" came from a vending machine, a far cry from their usual Christmas feast seated around their large dining room table surrounded by family and friends.

The Kucks are dedicated Christians, with a long-established history of ministry and serving. They had even founded a missions organization, TCCI/Teams Commissioned for Christ International. Yet despite their strong faith, Nathaniel's parents felt extremely isolated and emotionally bankrupt that Christmas. As they looked around the hospital ward, they observed that they weren't the only ones who were struggling to find any Christmas cheer amidst the sadness and loneliness of the sterile hospital environment. After all, a ward full of critically ill children tends to crush even the most optimistic attitude. They thought about all of the hospital staff who were also missing time with their families to serve others.

In that moment, they made a decision that would drastically change their lives. If Nathaniel wasn't in the hospital the next Christmas, they'd take action. The Kucks purposed in their hearts to find a way to encourage kids like Nathaniel and their families who were forced to spend Christmas in the hospital.

Following through on that pledge, the next Christmas, Nathaniel and the rest of the Kuck family returned to Arnold Palmer Children's Hospital in Orlando, Florida, accompanied by 40 other friends who wanted to spread the Christmas spirit. Bringing gifts of candy canes and homemade goodies, they filled the halls with Christmas carols and prayers for kids, their families and hospital staff. Their first Christmas outreach was so successful that it became an annual tradition called "Caroling for Kids."

Already, Nathaniel had earned the label of "miracle boy." Although he remained a nine-month-old baby developmentally, Nathaniel continually beat the odds and overcame tremendous physical obstacles. Cradled in his mother's arms, Nathaniel unexpectedly passed away on November 13, 2004, at only four years old. He was finally free from physical struggles, surgeries, feeding tubes and braces.

Even with the knowledge that Nathaniel was running around unencumbered on the streets of gold, in heaven with Jesus, that first Christmas after his death was very difficult for the Kuck family. Although Nathaniel had never been able to speak, walk or feed himself, in his short time on Earth he had already touched the hearts of all who knew and loved him. His parents deeply missed Nathaniel's captivating smile and the simple joy he brought to all who entered his world. The Kucks even temporarily considered canceling Caroling for Kids that Christmas. *It just wouldn't be the same without Nathaniel.* But the more they thought about it, the more they knew that Nathaniel wouldn't want them to stop reaching out to sick children and their families who especially needed the love of Jesus at Christmas.

Marie remembered back to a critical time more than 18 months earlier when she and Tim were feeling hopeless as they searched for a cure for their son's undiagnosed syndrome. After an unsuccessful attempt at one of the nation's top children's hospital, Nathaniel had undergone a successful surgery on his skull in Dallas. But then he contracted bacterial pneumonia that almost took his life. That's when an unknown nurse with tears streaming down her face approached the Kucks and asked if she could pray for them. Surprisingly, the nurse didn't pray for Nathaniel's healing. Instead she had prayed, "God, may Nathaniel's purpose in life be accomplished!"

Just a week after their son's death, the Kucks realized that God indeed had a greater purpose for Nathaniel. Through several different incidents, both Tim and Marie came to the same realization that Nathaniel's death wasn't supposed to be an ending, but merely a beginning. In 2002, inspired by their son's life, Tim and Marie officially launched Nathaniel's Hope, a nonprofit organization in his memory, dedicated to sharing hope with kids with special needs (whom they lovingly call VIP kids) and their families.

Their inaugural event was held on June 7, 2003, commemorating Nathaniel's birthday on June 6. Remembering Nathaniel's trademark smile, they called the event "Make 'm Smile." This now-annual fun-filled day serves a dual purpose of celebrating the lives of VIP kids and their families while also educating the public about special-needs children. Clowns, face painters, magicians and popular characters from Disney World, Sea World and Universal Studios help entertain the kids. The highlight of the day is the Buddy friendship stroll where families and individuals are invited to "be a buddy" to a VIP child and their family and walk around Lake Eola. It gives the public an opportunity to interact with special-needs families and overcome the typical fears and stereotypes often associated with disabled children. My friends Rich and Pam Crotty—he is mayor of Orange County, Florida—have embraced the program, as well as have numerous other elected officials and celebrities. It has truly become a yearly community event scheduled for the first Saturday of June.

In 2007, more than 5,000 people, including more than 700 VIPs, gathered around Orlando's Lake Eola to participate in "Make 'm Smile." During the festivities, more than 4,000 T-shirts, 5,000 Sea World hats, 3,500 Chick-fil-A sandwiches, 2,000 hotdogs, 20,000 drinks, Frito-Lay chips, snow cones, ice cream and cotton candy were given away. They even held a special butterfly release where families of VIP kids who have passed on to heaven were invited to release a butterfly in their child's memory.

"Caroling for Kids" has spread to other hospitals and is also an annual outreach of Nathaniel's Hope. In 2007, more than 500 volunteers formed 46 caroling teams to spread the joy of Christmas to 40 hospitals. Volunteers contributed more than 500 hours of help just preparing for the caroling event. A local school even adopted it as their community service project. And now the pilot program has started spreading to other cities, including Daytona Beach, Florida, and Atlanta, Georgia. In 2007, 57 Walgreens, in two Central Florida districts, partnered to collect toys for Nathaniel's Hope to distribute at

Christmas as they caroled. Each family is also given a booklet sharing Nathaniel's story and other stories of hope, as well as Christmas cookies and goodies to eat.

Caroling Caravan is a new outreach blessing VIP kids who are homebound and their families. Smaller teams of carolers drive to each home to sing Christmas carols, encourage and pray for them, and deliver gifts. The homebound families report that just the presence of the carolers is a blessing that makes their Christmas special.

Buddy Break is another outreach of Nathaniel's Hope. Tim and Marie knew from experience that parents who are caregivers of special-needs kids usually never receive a break from their endless responsibilities. They came up with a creative idea to partner with local churches to provide a free respite program designed to give parents of VIP kids a three-hour break once a month. During that time, each VIP kid is paired with a "Buddy" for one-on-one attention. While their caregivers enjoy a much-deserved break, the VIPs enjoy playing games, doing crafts, hearing inspiring children's stories, watching videos, listening to music, and much more. Their ultimate goal is to build a Buddy Break network across the nation that will assist families. Nathaniel's Hope offers training to other churches and communities who want to bring a Buddy Break to their city.

Through Buddy Break, God has further expanded the Kucks' dream to include a permanent facility where they can provide overnight or extended care to VIP families when they have a special need. Knowing that nothing is impossible with God, they are praying for donors to turn this dream into a reality.

Other ministries of Nathaniel's Hope include a National VIP Birthday Club, where they send a special birthday surprise each year to each VIP, and The Hall of Hope, honoring VIP kids who have relocated to their heavenly homes. Bearing Hope is a lovable plush beanie bear given to VIP kids to remind them of the hope they share.

Through the gift of Nathaniel's short life, Marie and Tim Kuck learned that there is value and purpose to every life and that things classified as imperfect by humans are actually perfect in the sight of God. Nathaniel taught them about unconditional love and perseverance. The cherished memories of his little handprints and the lessons that he taught them are forever imprinted on all of the Kucks' hearts. Nathaniel was a great showcase of God's faithfulness, and his memory propels his parents to fulfill God's purposes. Through their son's death, they continue to bring encouragement and life to others. Never underestimate the power of God to transform a tragedy into triumph. All it takes is your availability to dream God's dream. Marie and Tim will both testify that God continues to take their availability and ministry far beyond their wildest hopes. The key is discovering God's unique purpose and plan for you and living in your God-given passion.

If you have a VIP child or want to help spread Nathaniel's Hope to your church or city, please visit www.NathanielsHope.org or call (407) 857-8224. As other volunteers will tell you, the VIPs you serve actually end up blessing you more than you can give to them.

P. S. On September 5, 2006, Nathaniel's grandfather, Paul Kuck, founder of Regal Marine (one of the world's largest privately owned boat manufacturers) and one of the most godly businessmen I know, died. I've no doubt that Paul is in heaven, holding and playing with Nathaniel until Marie and Tim get a chance to hug their son again one day.

Hope is the good news of transforming grace now. We are freed not only from the fear of death but from the fear of life; we are freed for a new life, a life that is trusting, hopeful, and compassionate.

—BRENNAN MANNING

My *Weary* Child,

Be joyful in hope, patient in suffering and hardship, and faithful in prayer. During times of suffering, *remember* the One in whom you believe! Be convinced that I am able to guard everything you entrust to Me until that day. You can be 100 percent confident that I'll *faithfully* complete the good work I started in You and your family.

Filling You Up,

YOUR LIFE GIVER

(Romans 12:12; 2 Timothy 1:12; Philippians 1:6)

143

My *Anxious* Child,

Don't worry! Remember, I tenderly take care of the little birds, and you're much more important and valuable to Me.

Even before you were born, I *ordained* each and every one of your days.

My thoughts of you are precious! Let go of any *anxiety* that's robbing you of life and joy.

Instead, give everything to Me in prayer.

Then watch My peace that goes incredibly beyond all understanding. Guard your *heart* and your *mind* in Christ Jesus.

Providing All Your Needs,

YOUR FAITHFUL HEAVENLY FATHER

(Matthew 6:25-31; Psalm 139:16-17; Philippians 4:6-7)

Remembering Mary

NOT LONG AFTER HER WEDDING, Debbie started preparations in earnest to leave for the mission field with her husband, Richard. But during her annual physical, the doctor informed her that she might be pregnant, and the test soon confirmed it.

As her pregnancy progressed, Debbie asked her doctor what special arrangements she needed to make to deliver her baby overseas. When she explained that they were going to the mission field in Brazil, Debbie's doctor vigorously shook his head.

"No, you're not, Debbie! You can't go overseas. You won't be able to fly when your pregnancy is that far along." He also cautioned her that any doctor who delivered her baby needed to be familiar with her health record and possibility for complications. Debbie felt dazed and speechless. She returned home and told her husband the news. They had already raised all of their financial support to go to Brazil. Richard no longer had a job. He had been focusing all of his time on raising monetary support for their missions ministry. *Now what were they going to do for an income, and where would they live? And how would they pay for the hospital expenses for the baby's delivery without medical insurance?*

Richard and Debbie considered their situation and prayed about several options. Meanwhile, Richard applied for seminary and was accepted.

As Christmas approached, one of Debbie's friends, who was also pregnant, invited Debbie over for lunch and showed her their baby's nursery. The furnishings were complete, and the room was decorated in a Winnie the Pooh theme, with matching sheets, bumper pads, blankets and matching curtains. The nursery had everything you could dream of having for a baby.

Debbie was truly happy that her friend was so prepared for their coming baby, but she also began to sink into a bit of a pity party. *God, how come my friend has everything she needs when I don't even know where we're going to live?* She stopped at a store on the way home and bought a cheap onesie outfit for the baby so that she could at least say she had something for their first child.

That weekend, Richard and Debbie attended the Nativity play at their church. As Debbie watched Mary, the mother of Jesus, a light bulb turned on in her head. Debbie realized that Mary's life had a lot of unresolved questions as she waited to give birth to her son. Talk about an unexpected pregnancy! And she needed to find a place to deliver her Son. She didn't even rate a hospital. *No wonder Mary pondered all that the angel had told her!* Debbie focused on the fact that Mary had chosen to believe even though her future was uncertain.

As Debbie watched the rest of the play, God reminded her that He had always faithfully provided for her needs, and she could trust Him with the unknown details of this pregnancy, and each day, as she raised her family.

The day after Christmas, Richard and Debbie packed up the car and left the comfort of Florida to head for seminary in Fort Worth, Texas. God provided a great mobile home for them. They joined a wonderful and supportive Sunday school class. Later, their Sunday school class threw them a surprise baby shower, blessing them with everything they needed for their coming bundle of joy.

God even miraculously provided the medical expenses for the hospital. They discovered a local hospital that had a special plan for families in need.

Richard and Debbie didn't have to pay any medical expenses for their baby's delivery.

March 16, the day after their first wedding anniversary, they held baby Eric in their arms. As Debbie looked into her son's eyes, she thanked God for His absolute faithfulness. Although she didn't know what the future held, she *knew* she could fully trust the One who held their future.

Never be afraid to trust an unknown future to a known God.

−CORRIE TEN BOOM

My *Precious* Child,

Trust Me! I know the

plans I have for you.

My plans won't harm you;

they'll help you to thrive!

I'll make known to you the path of life

and fill you with joy in My *presence.*

You'll experience eternal pleasures

at My right hand.

Thinking of You,

YOUR GOD *of* HOPE

(Jeremiah 29:11; Psalm 16:11)

HEAVENLY FATHER,

Thank You for being my faithful Provider.
Forgive me for the times when I'm anxious or try
to fill my needs on my own. With easy credit, it's
so tempting to use the charge card for things that
I think we need and to get in over our heads in
debt. Show me the difference between my wants
and my needs. Don't let me fall into the "keeping
up with the Joneses" trap. Teach me to be content
in You. Remind me that You are all I need.
Help me to trust in You wholeheartedly and to
follow wherever You lead me.

My *Pain-Filled* Child,

In Me you *live* and *move*

and have your very being.

I haven't given you a spirit of fear.

Instead I've given you a spirit of *Sonship*.

My grace is all you need.

When you feel *weak*,

My power dwells in you.

Even if your flesh and your heart *fail*,

I'm the strength of your heart

and your portion forever.

Sustaining You,

YOUR GOD of LIFE

(Acts 17:28; Romans 8:15; 2 Corinthians 12:9; Psalm 73:26)

1995: The Best
and the worst
christmas

B E C K Y   B L A N K E N S H I P   C O U L D definitely relate to the first line
of Dickens's *A Tale of Two Cities*: "It was the best of times, it was the
worst of times . . ." She and her dear husband, Randy, had been blessed
with two beautiful girls: Beth was nine years old and Grace was six.

Randy was a successful attorney in the small central Florida town
where they lived. Becky was a stay-at-home mom. She had been cruising
through life at the hectic pace so prevalent in today's society, trying to
multi-task and keep up with all the responsibilities life demanded of her.
The Blankenship family attended church every Sunday morning
and Wednesday night. But without realizing it, they probably took
for granted all the blessings God had poured out on them
so consistently for many years until a devastating
diagnosis turned their world upside down.

In the spring of that year, Becky had
experienced an almost debilitating pain in
her right hip.

At times the pain was so intense that she wondered, *Lord, how can I go on living like this? It's so difficult to raise my girls with this pain.* Eventually the pain became too much for her to handle and she was forced to consult a doctor. He gave her a complete physical, including a mammogram, which came back negative. Over time, the hip pain eventually decreased. Becky was grateful that she could finally resume her normal activities.

That August, Becky and Randy celebrated their eighteenth wedding anniversary at a local restaurant. Becky was somewhat health conscious and normally excluded caffeine from her diet. But that night, she was enjoying celebrating alone with her husband and indulged in drinking several glasses of iced tea at dinner.

The next morning, she awoke discomforted by an intense pain shooting from her lower breast. When she examined the area, she discovered a large lump about a half inch in length. Becky couldn't believe it. Just three short months ago, her mammogram read negative.

They had already planned a trip to the west coast of Florida to celebrate their girls' great-grandmother's birthday, and were leaving that morning. So Becky postponed any further action concerning the lump.

When they returned home on a Monday, Becky called her gynecologist's office and told the nurse about the lump and how it had just popped up overnight. The nurse thought it sounded like a cyst, and recommended that Becky take 800 IUs of Vitamin E each day, and avoid caffeine. *Caffeine!!! That explains it,* Becky thought, remembering the caffeinated iced tea she drank the night before she had located the painful lump. She was relieved to hear that it was probably just a cyst.

The nurse also instructed Becky to call for an appointment if the lump didn't disappear. Soon after, Becky learned that doctors normally conduct a needle biopsy to determine if a lump is cancerous. Becky was dead set against any kind of a needle biopsy, due to her fear of needles.

But when the lump continued to grow at a rapid pace, Becky knew she didn't have a choice. She called her doctor and scheduled an appointment. Her doctor was very concerned by Becky's egg-sized lump and immediately referred her to a surgeon. The surgeon sent Becky for a second mammogram. Concerned by the results, the surgeon scheduled Becky for a radical mastectomy. Ironically, Becky insisted on a needle biopsy first before any action could be taken.

On Halloween day, Becky was leveled by the unexpected news that she had a very advanced and aggressive breast cancer. The surgeon scheduled a radical mastectomy for the next day. Becky and Randy immediately called another hospital to get a second opinion and were told to come at noon the next day for further testing.

Becky's young daughters had no idea what was going on and had already left for school that morning. She wrote a note to them explaining that they were on an adventure of faith and would see them soon. The girls' Grandma quickly offered to care for them while Becky and Randy were gone. None of them had any idea of the monumental eight-month adventure on which they were about to embark.

Becky underwent two months of very aggressive and powerful chemotherapy. Almost immediately, she lost all of her hair and experienced painful side effects, including extreme fatigue, nausea, headache and painful mouth sores, which made it difficult to eat or even swallow. Most of that time Becky was away from home staying with friends near the hospital, or actually hospitalized.

Randy valiantly picked up the slack and tackled the huge responsibilities of the house, caring for their girls and encouraging Becky through difficult therapy, on top of his demanding job as an attorney. Becky didn't realize the full extent of Randy's sacrifice until she started working at his office after she had completed eight months of treatment. Then she saw firsthand many of the responsibilities he dealt with on a daily basis and realized the extent of his sacrificial love during her battle with cancer.

Becky's faith remained strong, greatly attributable to the thousands of prayers that were lifted up on her behalf by so many friends, family and total strangers, some even from across the world. God's extended family blessed the Blankenship family in so many ways. Randy and Becky were so thankful and humbled by the absolute necessity to be on the receiving end of countless offers of help. So many people carried their family through the most trying season of their lives. They were blessed by the many wonderful people who stepped in to love and care for their little girls. Their church, their family and dear friends were selflessly there for them when they saw the need.

Needless to say, by Christmas of that year, Becky was pretty much a physical and emotional mess. Becky had almost forgotten the details of that Christmas until I asked her if she had a special Christmas story that I could share for this book. When Becky asked her oldest daughter about favorite Christmas memories, she was surprised when Beth, now 24 years old, brought up the Christmas that Becky battled cancer. Becky had blocked out much of that year because it was one of the hardest times of her life. But she was touched when Beth reminded her of the love and grace of God that were so exquisitely poured out to their family that Christmas.

Beth reminded her mom that their dear friends Cathy and her husband, Weegie, came over unexpectedly that Christmas morning and surprised them with hot cinnamon rolls, scrambled egg and sausage casserole, red napkins, Christmas silverware and all the fixings for a Christmas breakfast that's hard to forget.

Becky reflected on how much this act of kindness had meant to their family as they celebrated Christ's birth and life in 1995.

Beth smiled as she reminded her mom that she and her sister, Grace, had only received a few Dollar Store presents that year because understandably Becky and Randy didn't have the time or energy to do much shopping. Becky was visibly touched as Beth shared that it had been a special and fun

Christmas despite the lack of gifts. Beth was happy just to have her mom home that Christmas, knowing that she could very easily have died.

Becky thanked Beth for the reminder of God's love, which was awesomely poured out upon their family that Christmas of 1995. Yes, it had been the worst of times in many ways. Undergoing chemotherapy definitely is not one of her favorite memories. But looking back, by God's grace and with Beth's gentle reminder, she now realized that Christmas of 1995 was also the very best of times.

Let us remember that the Christmas heart is a giving heart,
a wide open heart that thinks of others first.

—George Matthew Adams

My *Healing* Child,

Don't be afraid, because I am your helper.

I will NEVER leave you or abandon you!

I've surrounded you with

people of faith. Get rid of anything stopping you

and run with endurance the race

I've already marked out for you!

In the midst of your struggles, the secret

is to *fix your eyes on Jesus*, the Author and

Perfecter of your faith. Remember how He

endured the cross for the joy that was to come.

Cheering You on to Victory,

YOUR HEAVENLY FATHER

(Hebrews 13:5b-6; Hebrews 12:1-3)

DEAR HEAVENLY FATHER,

Sometimes I just get too busy for my own good. I need Your help to simplify my life. Remind me that You are my confidence. Show me where I need to cut back. Let Your Word be a light to my path. Help me trust in You more.

My **Prayerful** Child,

Don't parents *give* good

gifts to their children?

Even more so, I love to *give* good gifts

when My children ask. Think about it.

If I didn't even spare My own Son for you,

won't I *graciously* give you good things?

I'll satisfy your desires.

Blessing You,

YOUR FATHER GOD

(Matthew 7:11; Romans 8:32; Psalm 103:5)

A Home to Bless and Be Blessed

REBEKAH WAS DRIVING HOME from Christmas at her husband's parents' house. After her husband, John, dozed off and their children slept soundly in the back of the car, Rebekah took advantage of the quiet to reflect and spend time with God.

Over the years, she had developed a deep and consistent personal relationship and friendship with her heavenly Father. She had learned the secret of being content with whatever God gave her.

But that snowy Christmas night, during a sweet time of conversation with God, Rebekah felt the freedom to share her heart's desire with her Best Friend: She wanted to own a home again.

During her childhood, Rebekah had lived in church parsonages. In her early marriage, she had lived in rental properties. She'd try to personalize each house, but there was always the remembrance that these places really weren't her homes. She dreamed of being able to decorate in the way she wanted to without having to submit to a barrage of questions or a committee's decision. Like a sparrow looking for a nest, Rebekah longed for a home of her own again like they had when their children were babies.

Some people teach "name it and claim it" prosperity gospel. But Rebekah has always believed the importance of loving God for who He is, not for what He gives or does. She realized that owning a home was a blessing, not a necessity. She reflected on how Mary and Joseph were "homeless" during their Bethlehem trip and couldn't even find a room to rent for Jesus' birth.

She prayed, "Heavenly Father, I know there are a lot of homeless people. And I'm very grateful for the housing You've graciously provided us. But if it's Your will, would You please bless us again with a home of our own?"

Trying to pray specifically, she continued, "Lord, my dream home would have plenty of room for company, and a big yard . . ."

As she drove down a street in Kewanee, Illinois, Rebekah pointed to a large Victorian house that caught her attention. "Lord, I'd really be blessed if our house had interesting character architecturally like that house."

Rebekah continued her sweet fellowship with God until she pulled into the driveway of their rental house.

Six months later, John brought home some flyers with houses for sale. Rebekah was immediately drawn to one of the houses, a Victorian. They quickly called the realtor and set up an appointment. Rebekah wanted the large Victorian house. But since she had thoroughly studied the market, she knew the house was overpriced and made a lower offer.

Surprisingly, the sellers accepted their offer. After John and Rebekah signed the closing papers, she pulled up in front of the house and parked. Something about it looked oddly familiar.

His voice wasn't audible, but God's Spirit nudged her and whispered, "Remember?"

Rebekah hadn't noticed it until then, but this was the *very* house "with character" she had pointed to six months earlier.There was no doubt in Rebekah's mind that God had blessed her with the very desire of her heart. Each Christmas, she continues to thank God for the gift of their home. With the 14 rooms, plus 8 additional rooms in the basement, their home has become a home away from home to many people, including me. I've witnessed firsthand that the Montgomery home is one of hospitality, fellowship, refreshment and encouragement that overflows with God's blessings and love to others.

The main purpose of prayer is not to make life easier,
nor to gain magical powers, but to know God.

—PHILIP YANCEY

My *Delightful* Child,

You can be *confident* that I hear you when you **ask** according to My will.

I'm your *Sun* and your *Shield*.

I give you favor and honor.

When your life is *blameless*,
I bless you with good things.

As you *delight* yourself in Me,
I *give* you the things
that your heart truly desires.

Favoring You,

YOUR KING *of* KINGS

(1 John 5:14-15; Psalm 84:11; Psalm 37:4)

DEAR HEAVENLY FATHER,

I want to love You for who You are, not only for what You do or give. Thank You that You hear me even before I call. I confess that sometimes my prayers are selfish and all about me. I want to seek Your will. But sometimes it's so hard to distinguish between Your will and my desires. Help me choose Your will— nothing more, nothing less, nothing else. I want to desire the things You want me to seek after, because You always know what's best for me. And know that I'm looking forward to dwelling with You forever.

My *Compassionate* Child,

When you are *kind* to those in need,

you honor Me. I was hungry and you fed Me.

I was *thirsty* and you gave Me a *drink*

You invited Me in when I was a stranger.

You gave Me clothes. When I was sick,

you took care of Me. You *visited* Me in prison.

Remember, when you've served the least

of these, you've actually served Me!

Calling You to Service,

YOUR HEAVENLY FATHER

(Proverbs 14:31; Matthew 25:35-45)

A cup of water in His Name

MY FRIEND JOE HURSTON is an amazing entrepreneur and man of faith. He founded Air Mobile Ministries in 1978. For years he's been a missionary pilot and formerly ran a mission in Haiti with his wife, Cindy. While they were serving in Haiti, he started refilling toner cartridges for their ministry's use because cartridges were hard to find and very expensive. Then others started asking him to refill their cartridges too. He used the extra money to help support their ministry. One thing led to another and eventually he started Cartridge Source of America, picking up clients like Office Max and NASA.

One major problem that Joe and Cindy continually battled in Haiti was lack of clean water, especially after hurricanes and flooding. Usually during disasters, Joe flew thousands of gallons of bottled water in. But water is extremely heavy and bulky to transport. In June 2004, after terrible flooding on the Haiti-Dominican border, more than 3,000 people lost their lives. Joe called his friend Rolf Englehard, who had invented the Vortex Voyager Water Machine with the world-renowned chemist Dr. Howard Malmstadt. Each Vortex is a first-responder rapid response able to purify 22 to 25 gallons of water per hour using less energy than a 60-watt light bulb!

Joe rounded up as many Vortex Voyagers as he could and headed to Haiti. Just three months later, Tropical Storm Jeanne hit Haiti, and another 3,000 Haitians were lost due to flooding. Again, Joe's team returned with more Vortex Voyagers. The trips were so successful that it prompted Joe to contact Rolf about the possibility of partnering to mass-produce the Vortex Voyagers. They set up a plant in Titusville, Florida, and the first units were finished December 15, 2004. Joe and Cindy knew that the Lord had powerful plans for this remarkable tool to save lives.

On December 19, Joe attended his church in the Space Coast of Florida after recently returning from humanitarian flights to Haiti. Midway through the service, as he and Cindy sat in the back of the church, Joe's eyes drifted to the side of the sanctuary.

It was as if someone had placed a big-screen TV right in front of him. God surprised him with an unusual vision. In perfect high-definition clarity, he observed a multitude of people. Joe was sitting on the beach looking at a sea of people. As he looked closer, he noticed that the faces were clearly the faces of Muslims who were dying of thirst.

In this vision, Joe and his wife were squatting down in servant positions, with their water purifier, serving water to the Muslims one cup at a time. The people appeared to be thankful.

Suddenly, a powerful and violent man came up to Joe and got right up to his face. He harshly questioned Joe in a threatening way, "Who sent you here?"

Joe knew that he had to choose his words carefully. He paused before saying, "Jesus sent me here." In the vision, the man stopped and bowed his face. Pausing for a few seconds, he then said, "Thank You, Jesus," and the vision was gone. The whole vision lasted no more than 25 seconds, but there was no doubt in Joe's mind that he had just witnessed something supernatural.

Joe and Cindy's ministry had always been centered around the Caribbean. He was excited about the prospect of reaching out to Muslims. He gently poked his wife. At first she whispered, "Shh . . ." trying to listen to the pastor's message. But after Joe whispered, "Cindy, I just had a vision," she turned toward him. After 14 years of marriage, Cindy knew that something was urgent.

Relieved that they were sitting in the back of the church, Cindy whispered, "What was the vision?"

After Joe explained the odd happenings, Cindy said, "Cool. We've never ministered to a Muslim population before."

After the service, Joe spotted his pastor in the back of the church. Joe stopped him as he was leaving to prepare for the next service and briefly recapped the unique happenings. His pastor raised his finger and said, "I believe that vision was from God. Be prepared."

Christmas was on Saturday. Sunday morning, Joe woke up early and felt a strange prompting to check the world news on the Internet. That's when he first learned about the massive earthquake and resulting tsunami in Southeast Asia. First reports were coming in that 1,200 had died. But as he sat there, the death toll kept rising—12,000 . . . then 30,000.

That afternoon, after Joe returned home from church, a reporter friend from Channel 9 (ABC News Affiliate) who had gone on a relief mission to Haiti with Joe called to see if Joe had heard about the devastating 9.3 earthquake. The reporter further inquired if Joe was going to go to the area affected by the tsunami.

Joe said yes, strongly sensing that God wanted him there, but not knowing how he was going to finance the trip or get enough Voyagers produced. The manufacturing plant was still making adjustments to the Voyager but volunteered to work night and day to move up production so that Joe could take 20 units to the region that was in such dire need of drinking water.

Incredibly, on January 8, Joe and Cindy boarded a commercial plane for Indonesia. Forty hours and several connections later, they landed in Medan, Northern Sumatra, the staging area for worldwide relief efforts. In that city, there were few visible signs of damage. Most relief teams were trying to get to Banda Aceh. But Joe felt led to go to Meleuboh instead. John Goheen, an award-winning newsman with 15 Emmys to his name, had volunteered to film the disaster but didn't think that was possible because of the location and the known terrorism in that area. Not to mention that there were already 2,000 other people ahead of them on the waiting list for the helicopter or other transportation.

Not backing down, Joe replied, "John, I don't know how we'll do it, but I just believe that we're supposed to go there."

That night Joe couldn't sleep. With so many people in desperate need of water, there had to be some way to cut through the bureaucratic red tape so that he could start purifying water. As he prayed and agonized, God gave him a plan.

The next morning, Joe emptied the garbage can provided in his room and filled it with dirty water. He took the garbage can full of water and one of the Vortex Voyagers to the hotel lobby. After a quick one-minute set-up, Joe started purifying the water with the 20-pound Vortex Voyager and giving drinks to people in the lobby.

Someone influential must have been impressed, because Joe and his crew of seven were moved near the front of the waiting list. The next morning, they were on the Singapore Armed Forces Chinook helicopter flying over the 12,000-foot mountains en route to Meleuboh. From the air, they viewed pockets of water everywhere. There were newly formed lakes and bodies of water where towns used to be. Some places looked as if they had been struck by a nuclear bomb.

On the ground, they witnessed gruesome sights. Rescuers found more than 1,000 bodies a day floating through the water. Although Joe has witnessed some phenomenal disasters, he had never witnessed such an extensive loss of life before. Joe and his team rapidly set up operations and had 20 Vortex Voyagers in operation at the hands of other relief organizations. These units saved many lives.

As Joe and Cindy and their team gave away cups and gallons of water, they heard unbelievable stories of loss and miracles. One of the girls they served lost 400 members of her family in the tsunami. In her village alone, 32,000 of the 42,000 people there perished. As she was running away, she saw the waves carry people all around her away. They heard similar stories their entire trip. So many people shared that they had lost 30 or 40 members of their family. The Hurstons felt so privileged to be able to reach and love these survivors by giving them a cup of water in Jesus' name.

When Joe recounted his trip to me, he expressed how grateful the people of Indonesia were of anyone who showed up to help. The villagers were amazed that so many people came. Joe noted that the Muslims were astounded at the speed, sincerity and depth of the Christian Church's help in their time of need. As the Hurstons served, so many said, "We thought you [Christian Americans] hated us; why did you come?"

Joe simply replied, "The Jesus whom I love and serve loves you and clearly told me to bring water to you." Joe thought back to that earlier vision and thanked Jesus for the opportunity to bring water in His name.

The 2004 tsunami in Indonesia was the deadliest storm in more than 200 years, with a death toll of over 229,000. Joe made a second trip to South East Asia in April 2005, delivering another 30 units. Since the 2004 tsunami, Joe has helped deploy more than 600 Vortex Voyager units around the world, all of which were donated, thanks to generous donors. In May 2008, he took the lifesaving machines to Myanmar, where 2.5 million survivors faced dehydration, starvation, homelessness and the threat of deadly diseases after the devastating cyclone. He's demonstrated the machine before the United Nations, the Red Cross, USAID (United States Agency for International Development) and many NGOs (non-government organizations). And the documentary that John Goheen filmed of Joe's team in action has aired on HDNet World Report more than eight times worldwide.

My *Servant* Child,

Remember that you're a light to the world. When they see your *good works,* they'll praise Me.

My *Spirit* is upon you. I've anointed you to preach the good news to the meek; to bind up the brokenhearted, to proclaim *liberty* to the captives and to proclaim acceptance; to comfort those who mourn; to give them *beauty* for ashes, the oil of joy for mourning; to use the spirit of praise to lift their heaviness.

With You Always,

YOUR KING *of* KINGS

(Matthew 5:14,16; Isaiah 61:1-3)

DEAREST FATHER:

I want to serve others for you this holiday.
Make me aware of opportunities to be a
bright light for You in my community.
Help me to see needs and step in to fill the
gaps. Remind me that as I'm serving
others, I'm really serving You. Don't let
me just serve, but help me to reach out to
others in need with an inviting smile that
expresses their value to You and to me.
Thanks that You so graciously serve me
even though you are King of kings.

My *Special* One,

You have a treasured place in My heart.

I'm a *father* to the fatherless

and a *defender* of widows.

Never forget that I'm the ultimate

source of every good and perfect *gift* you receive.

You can always count on Me,

because I never *change*.

Be transformed by renewing your

mind so that you can prove what My will is.

I want you to know what is

good, acceptable and *perfect*.

Giving Good Gifts,

YOUR FATHER *of* HEAVENLY LIGHTS

(Psalm 68:5; James 1:17; Romans 12:2)

the christmas plate

BY LATE AFTERNOON ON December 24, the chipped ceramic plaque was the lone item remaining on the discounted Christmas display at the local Hallmark store. Its artificial holly attached at the top was twisted and dusty. And as if it didn't already look pitiful enough, a dollop of glue revealed a bald spot where remnants of a red plaid ribbon remained. Barely glancing at the cursive font, and paying equally little attention to the words in script, April picked up the plaque to claim it as hers. With Christmas only days away, she and her three preschool-age children were all but homeless, heartsick and fast running out of hope.

Pulling four crumpled dollar bills and change from her purse to pay the cashier, April held her purchase tenderly to her chest, knowing there would be no gifts this year bearing her name. And somehow, inexplicably, holding this small broken treasure offered her comfort. Yet, as she began reading the words on the plaque, she felt her brave front—her best-ever false bravado—crumbling not only before her eyes, but also before all those last-minute shoppers as well. Blinking back tears as they spilled down her face, April darted through the mall and out the exit to the safety of her well-worn van.

And much like a Hallmark holiday movie, complete with strains of familiar Christmas carols drifting softly though the crisp air, scenes from her young family's life played in her heart. She wondered, *How was it possible that her once-prominent family, ripe with promise and blessings beyond their wildest dreams, was now battered, bruised and broken seemingly beyond all repair?* She barely recognized the husband and wife as scenes from earlier in their marriage played in her heart. They were young, carefree and relaxed. Ah, the promise of youth!

With little warning (as usually occurs!), babies filled their home in rapid succession. And with the pitter-patter of little feet came an abundance of professional, as well as personal, blessings. Indeed, life for this young family was notably charmed, and the world, and all it had to offer, was theirs for the taking.

Now back at her parents' home and slumped in an oversized chair, April felt the familiar but unforgiving heartache she experienced each time she relived the physical and emotional breakdown of her young husband. Each month brought with it yet another new symptom, an updated diagnosis, additional hospital stays and altered lifestyle. But soon the months turned into one year, then two. The details, that need not be discussed, were unspeakable. The pain, unbearable. And though their love was born out of God's blessing, and they vowed valiantly that they could and would go the distance with their marriage, sometimes even love is not enough to withstand the ravages of illness. And so the single strand that held their life together strained. When April's husband died, she was on her own to pick up the pieces of her family's very broken life. Much to her dismay, she discovered that their beautiful mansion and almost everything they owned was mortgaged to the hilt. She walked away with little more than her children and their clothes.

Still nestled in the old armchair, her tears abruptly stopped as her life's "journey" took on a new concern: it was four days until Christmas; it felt like her family had been gutted with a machete and their old life ripped from them with no hint and little hope of where or what tomorrow might hold.

April lifted the ceramic plaque from its bag, reading the words with slow deliberation:

> Christmas is eternal
> like the love
> that gave it birth~
> like the love
> that touches others
> as it reaches 'round the earth.

Suddenly, a hint of hope brushed across her weary heart. Though the *feeling* was fleeting, indeed, hope had, if only for a moment, stirred within her heart. Then April returned to the reality that Christmas would be their most painful one, one she secretly wished she could wish away. Again, as if drawn to the very words on that cracked plaque, she felt a flicker of hope followed by a sense of peace. Within minutes, the pitter-patter of little feet alerted her that her little ones had awakened from afternoon naps.

Thank goodness for Mom and Dad taking us in until we can come up with a plan for part two of our lives. And Mom has been a true blessing, watching the children as often as possible, April thought, as the children snuggled into her. But her family's finances were lean, and the last time she checked, "love" wouldn't provide even a modest Christmas for her children . . . that is, until a single act of *agape* love from an anonymous giver taught her otherwise.

It was the late afternoon of December 23. A ribbon of smoke circled from the old brick chimney when the mailman dropped an envelope bearing April's name through the mail slot. Mindlessly, she tore open the envelope that offered no return address, and a handwritten note and check in the amount of $1,000 fluttered to the floor. On the note, the bearer of the gift wrote:

I pray this gift will help you and your babies this Christmas.

Christmas blessings,
A friend

Many years later, April shared with me that she cannot recall just how long she sat in stunned silence. Or how long it was that she wept. But as a freshly fallen mantle of snow silently blanketed the earth, April's eyes were drawn to the chipped plaque on the table nearby. And wiping tears away as quickly as they fell, she struggled to read aloud, one more time, the words that would forever change her life:

> Christmas is eternal
> like the love
> that gave it birth~
> like the love
> that touches others
> as it reaches 'round the earth.

It was at that moment she understood why she was drawn to that cracked plaque. For though it was dusty, chipped *and* defective, its words told the *truest* meaning of Christmas! Just as Christ's love for us is eternal and is the very reason we celebrate the season, so too it is His children who reach out to those bruised, broken and beaten down by life's unspeakable tragedies. And so it was a gift of God's love, unribboned, unboxed, and completely unexpected that restored April's faith in Her heavenly father, her fellow man and her family's future.

In her prayer of thanksgiving, April prayed—and this, indeed, was the beginning of part two of their lives—that the Lord would find favor on her so that she might do for other single mothers what an "angel" had done for her.

My dear friend April, whose name has been changed to protect the anonymous nature of her donations, received that unexpected but much needed blessing more than 20 years ago. I've often wondered if that unknown angel has any idea how much he or she impacted my girlfriend's life at such a critical time.

Shortly after that amazing Christmas gift, God brought an incredible godly husband into my friend's life. God's favor has truly shined on their union. Living a life rich with faith, family, fellowship and friends, April and her husband have generously used their finances to bless others in need throughout the year.

That act of kindness at April's greatest time of need sparked a family tradition. Each Christmas, God faithfully directs April to a single mom in dire need of a blessing. She looks for a mom who is weary and worn, whose faith is faltering through circumstances beyond her control. A single mom who needs hope stirred within her heart again and is in desperate need of a Christmas miracle. Then April writes a Christmas check to that family, usually with an anonymous note retelling the story of the anonymous angel that blessed her family at her greatest time of need. Writing and sending that check is one of April's greatest joys each Christmas.

I love it when she tells me the story behind each year's recipient, and I wish that I somehow could be a fly on the wall to see that mom's face light up as she opens the envelope that will rekindle her belief that God *truly* provides every need.

Even though April has many priceless possessions and jewels today, that well-worn ceramic plaque is still one of my friend's most beloved possessions. To her it is a tender yet timeless reminder that Christ's love *is* eternal.

When we pass on His message of hope and love to others, we're helping to spread that blessing 'round the earth and perhaps even inspiring others to continue that chain of love.

My *Orphaned* Child,

I've called you, and I'm faithful.

I won't leave you comfortless;

I'll come to you. Give Me all of your

cares, because I deeply care for you.

Because of My grace, I became poor

so that you might become *rich*.

When you prioritize My kingdom

and *righteousness* as first, I'll take care of

all of your needs. I won't let the chil-

dren of the righteous go without.

Eternally,

JESUS

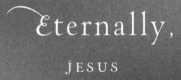

(1 Thessalonians 5:24; John 14:18; 1 Peter 5:7; 2 Corinthians 8:9;
Matthew 6:33; Psalm 37:25)

DEAREST HEAVENLY FATHER,
*Remind me that You're behind every good thing
I ever receive. Thank You for Your absolute
goodness. You are my Good Shepherd!
Make me totally dependent on You. When I
get bogged down with stinking thinking and
want to have a pity party, help me renew my
mind with the promises of Your eternal Word.
Thanks for Your faithfulness that continues to
all generations, and that You lead me in
paths of righteousness.*

My *Heartbroken* Child,

when you focus on Me,

you'll *discover* My perfect *peace*.

When you *suffer*,

My comfort overflows.

My *promise preserves* your life.

Loving My Word

leads you to great peace.

Graciously,

YOUR GOD

(Isaiah 26:3; 2 Corinthians 1:5; Psalm 119:50)

*Whatever clouds your face today, ask Jesus, the light of the world,
to help you look behind the cloud to see His glory and His plans for you.*

— BILLY GRAHAM

The Gift of a Lifetime

LITTLE CARRIE ALLEN KNEW that she couldn't have sweets like the other children could. Normally, she followed her strict diet. At only three years old, a visit to the family doctor had revealed that Carrie was diabetic and would require insulin shots for the rest of her life.

In December 1949, Carrie went to first grade the last day before Christmas break without any signs of illness. After school, Carrie ran home. Running up the stairs into the kitchen, her big blue eyes were aglow as she hid something behind her back. Extending the wrapped gift forward, Carrie excitedly blurted out, "I made it just for you, Mommy."

Visibly touched, her mom smiled and replied, "Thank you so much, dear. I can't wait to see what you made me. But let's put it aside so I can enjoy opening your special gift at Christmas next week."

The next day, Carrie developed flu-like symptoms. Lillian realized that even the flu was serious for a diabetic child. She stayed up with Carrie all Saturday night after her daughter started vomiting. Lillian kept cooling down Carrie's feverish head with a wet towel. While putting some clean clothes away in Carrie's dresser drawers, Lillian discovered some hidden candy canes that Carrie must have snuck from her class Christmas party.

Sunday morning, Carrie's condition rapidly deteriorated. Lillian called a baby-sitter while her husband, Joe, borrowed a car to rush their little girl to the hospital in Chicago.

"Mommy, am I going to die?" Carrie asked with fear in her voice as they drove to the hospital.

"Sweetheart, don't worry," Lillian said in a calm, reassuring voice. "You're not going to die. But even if you did, heaven is a beautiful place. The streets are made of gold and there are no shots or sickness there." She decided to give Carrie the doll they had brought for her early Christmas present so that she wouldn't feel so alone in the hospital.

At the hospital, Carrie's regular doctor was off rounds for the holidays. A young intern looked in on Carrie instead. Seeing how sick little Carrie was, the intern knew he couldn't leave for his Christmas party before his young patient was stabilized. Lillian heard him impatiently make several calls, apologizing that he couldn't leave for the party yet.

Carrie cried when her parents had to leave at 10:30 that night to go home to check on their other four young children.

By the time they got home and took the baby-sitter home, they were exhausted. After midnight, the phone rang. Lillian wondered if Carrie needed to hear her voice of reassurance again. After all, the hospital was a scary place to be left alone when you're little. Lillian wearily answered the phone and discovered that it was the hospital.

"Mrs. Allen, did you bring in a young diabetic daughter for treatment today?"

"Yes," replied Mrs. Allen, never expecting what came next.

"Your daughter expired. She went into insulin shock and we couldn't bring her back. We need you to return to the hospital immediately to identify the body." The voice on the other end of the phone gave the news in such a matter-of-fact tone that Lillian was silenced in utter shock.

After a few moments, she said, "We'll be there as soon as we can. But we have to find a sitter to stay with our other children."

She hung up the phone and tearfully told her husband the shocking news. They sat there, numb. When Carrie had asked if she was going to die that morning, Lillian had never even considered that possibility.

After a neighbor from a few blocks away arrived, the Allens went to the hospital. Together they identified their young daughter's lifeless body. The older nurse cruelly said to Lillian, "She's better off."

Later, they learned that in a rush to leave for his party, the young intern had accidentally given Carrie a lethal insulin overdose of almost 400 units on an empty stomach.

It's never easy to make funeral arrangements for a child, especially at Christmas. At the funeral parlor, Psalm 18:30 kept coming back to Lillian's mind:

As for God, his way is perfect: the word of the LORD is tried: he is a buckler to all those that trust in him (Psalm 18:30, *KJV*).

Carrie was buried just two days before Christmas. She looked so peaceful in the pretty pink dress with a pink bow in her hair. She looked like she was just sleeping. As she walked away in the snow from that tiny-sized white casket, Lillian felt as if a part of her own body had been ripped away.

Lillian knew that God had given her and Joe their five children, and it was God's right to take Carrie home to Himself. But she questioned why Carrie had to die before Christmas. Somehow God gave the Allens the grace to explain to their other four children that their sister was now in heaven with Jesus.

On Christmas morning, Lillian and Joe tried to smile for the sake of their other children who eagerly ripped the paper off their presents. Lillian watched them joyfully play with their toys, not understanding the tragedy that she and Joe were dealing with. When Lillian knew that she couldn't hide her tears much longer, she quietly slipped out of the Christmas mayhem into the solitude of her room and wept alone as she recited Bible verses.

Although Lillian and Joe chose not to sue the hospital for the intern's negligence, Lillian blamed his careless mistake for their daughter's death. *Why did he have to be in such a rush to leave for that stupid party?* Lillian sunk into a deep pity party as the questions and doubts flooded her mind.

Overwhelmed by grief, she soaked the sheets with her tears. After a few minutes, she heard God's still, small voice remind her of Isaiah 26:3, a verse she had memorized: "Thou wilt keep him in perfect peace whose mind is stayed on Thee, because He trusteth in Thee."

God's Word gently communicated to Lillian's heartbroken soul that she had no peace because she wasn't keeping her mind focused on Him. Instead, she had let the circumstances of Carrie's sudden death distract her from that focus. *If God's way was perfect, who was she to question His timing?* She realized that she had tried to put question marks where God had placed a period.

The next morning, the sun shone brightly. Lillian still deeply missed Carrie, but she went to her piano and played this song in faith:

> Trust in the Lord and don't despair, He is a friend so
> true. No matter what your troubles are, Jesus will see
> you thru. Sing when the day is bright, sing in the darkest
> night. Every day, all the way, I will sing, sing, sing.

Lillian finally remembered the gift that Carrie had eagerly given her to open at Christmas. She regretted that she hadn't given Carrie the joy of seeing her open it. Lillian cried as she looked at the homemade calendar her young daughter had made. She cherished it, knowing that she'd never receive another gift from Carrie in this life. The rest of the year, the calendar was a daily reminder of Carrie's love.

Lillian's two-year-old daughter, Patti, was a part of the healing process. Whenever Patti would sense that her mommy was sad, she'd come up to her and say, "Mommy, don't cry. Carrie in heaven with Jesus."

The week between Christmas and New Year's, WYCO, the company Joe worked for, always hosted a dinner for its employees at a hotel in downtown Chicago. Lillian didn't want to go, but friends convinced her that she needed to get out of the house.

At the employee dinner, the Allens were seated across the table from a young couple that Lillian had never met. The couple had heard of Carrie's death and expressed their sympathy.

Several years later, in April 1953, Joe came home from work and said, "Honey, remember Mac and Helen Correa, that couple we sat across the table from at the Christmas party after Carrie died? I just heard that their only child died of a kidney disease." He continued, "I think we should go to the funeral parlor in West Chicago."

At first, Lillian didn't want to go. She couldn't bear to see another child in a small coffin. But Joe convinced her that they could give the Correas hope.

As soon as Lillian and Joe walked through the doors of the funeral parlor, Helen recognized Lillian and said, "Mrs. Allen, how did you ever live through the loss of your daughter?"

Lillian teared up as she told Helen, "It's still hard at times, and I'll always miss her, but without the Lord and the promises of His Word, I never could have dealt with the pain of losing our Carrie. I'm so sorry about the loss of your son."

With a shared understanding of the incredible loss of the death of a child, they warmly embraced for a few moments.

About a week after their son, Jerry's, funeral, Helen received an invitation in the mail from Lillian to come for lunch. At first she thought about declining, as she wasn't ready for socializing, not to mention that the Allens had seemed too religious at that company party years earlier. But then she unfolded the beautiful stationery and began to read . . .

He is a little flower
plucked from this world of woe.
He will blossom in God's garden,
and by His love will grow.
Left from the evil of this world,
his life shall perfect be,
Dwelling in the mansions all through eternity.

Oft times our hearts are troubled,
and oft we wonder why
Our little ones from heaven
must leave our homes and die.
And yet we cannot think of them as dead—
but just away.
For they are with our blessed Lord
forever more to stay.

So when your heart is heavy
And sorrows bend you low,
In the secret of His presence,
You'll find a heavenly glow.
He will give you new strength for every day
And all our sorrows share.
So weep not loved ones for him;
He's in our Savior's care.

Lillian Allen had composed the beautiful poem after Carrie's death; now its words had been modified in memory of Helen's son, Jerry. Touched by the poem, and desperately seeking any relief from her unbearable grief, Helen decided to accept the lunch invitation.

After their pleasant luncheon, Lillian opened her Bible and started sharing the hope of God's wonderful promises with Helen.

For the Son of Man came to seek and to save what was lost (Luke 19:10).

He that believeth on the Son hath everlasting life (John 3:36).

In him we have redemption through his blood, the forgiveness of sins, in accordance with the riches of God's grace (Ephesians 1:7).

For the wages of sin is death, but the gift of God is eternal life in Christ Jesus our Lord (Romans 6:23).

In my Father's house are many rooms. . . . I am going there to prepare a place for you. . . . I will come back and take you to be with me that you also may be where I am (John 14:2-3).

That day, in my Grandma Allen's living room, Helen received the greatest gift she would *ever* receive when she invited Jesus into her heart and accepted God's gift of eternal life. Seven years later, Helen had the joy of leading her husband, and later, all of her immediate family, to a personal relationship with Jesus.

Helen constantly shared her faith when she'd meet a stranger or speak at women's luncheons. Over the years she has experienced the joy of leading many to accept God's gift of Salvation. Helen's daughter, Melinda Schmidt, went on to become a Christian radio host on Moody Bible Institute's WMBI and encourages thousands across the country through her faith.

I haven't met my Aunt Carrie yet. But I've been truly blessed by my grandmother's legacy of faith. Many years after Carrie's death, when I was six years old, Carrie's sister, my mom, died. My dear grandma taught us that song that she had played on the piano in faith in her time of grief. Whenever we thought my dad was sad, we'd start singing, "Trust in the Lord and don't despair . . ." We sang that song so much, I'm sure that my dad thought we were broken records.

My personal faith in God has sustained me through many crises and disappointments. And because I accepted God's gift of salvation when I was five,

I'm looking forward to a big reunion with my mom, my Grandpa Allen, my Grandpa and Grandma Weiss, Papa Martens, Uncle George, and many others. I'm sure that my mom or Grandma Allen will finally introduce me to Aunt Carrie in heaven one day.

If you haven't accepted God's gift yet, I urge you to receive Jesus as your personal Savior this Christmas. He's the best present you'll ever receive. Celebrating His birth and the good news of His gift to the world is the true meaning of Christmas. Whenever you draw close to Him, He promises that you'll experience His Presence and His perfect peace.

Being at peace with yourself is a direct result
of finding peace with God.

—OLIN MILLER

My *Tender* Child,

Despite what you may feel,

I'm never slow in keeping My promise.

I'm longsuffering toward you and others because

I'm not willing that anyone should perish.

It's My *desire* for everyone to come to repentance.

Don't let your hearts be troubled or be afraid.

Trust in God and trust in Me too.

My Father's house has many mansions and I've gone ahead

to *prepare* a place for you. I am your Way, your Truth,

and your Life—your one and only bridge to God. No one

comes to Him except through Me. *I give you My peace,*

which offers you confident assurance in any circumstance.

I comfort you in all your trials so that you can

comfort others who are troubled with the comfort you've

received from Me. One day *you'll be with Me.*

Waiting for you,

JESUS, YOUR PRINCE *of* PEACE

(2 Peter 3:9; John 14:1-6,27; 2 Corinthians 1:3-4)

DEAR FATHER,

Your way is perfect and Your Word is totally flawless. It's not fun to suffer. When I'm in the midst of a major trial, help me see past the present circumstances. Help me trust in You wholeheartedly, knowing that You see the end result. As You comfort Me, please help me reach out with Your hope to others. Thanks that You can take the bad things in my life that I wouldn't have chosen and use them to benefit me and others. Great is Your faithfulness!

acknowledgments

SPECIAL THANKS TO: My mom and dad; Tremendous Charlie Jones (King of Hugs); R. C. Sproul; John Maxwell; Wally Bronner (and Bronner's CHRISTmas Wonderland); Shantel Davis; Shelly and Angelo Ballestero; Charlotte Hale; Kris, Mike and Michael Langston; Coni and Doug Rhudy; Richard and Debbie Lord; Becky Blakenship; Marie and Tim Kuck; Nathaniel's Hope; Brienne and Heather Murk; Nikki and Jeremy Campbell (thanks for your sacrifice to defend our country); Belinda Elliott; Joe and Cindy Hurston; Rebekah Montgomery; the Dominguez Family and Lisa Sams and Brian Clarke; and Marcia Hepworth for allowing me to tell your stories.

To my family (Sharon and Kip, Steve and Tammy, Sarah and Victor, and my eight cool nephews and nieces): thanks for your love and encouragement and patience through deadlines.

My sister Pat—you've been much more than just a sister and roommate to me. Thanks for serving me and loving me behind the scenes for so many years. Know that you are the wind beneath my wings. I can never thank you enough.

Uncle Paul and Aunt Norma Weiss (you're always there to encourage me).

My Orlando support team—Angelo and Shelly Ballestero, and Dave and Mary Ellen Murray: You guys ROCK! What a force of talent and creativity! I've been so inspired by knowing you, praying together, and worshiping God with you. Shelly, it's been an extra joy working through our deadlines together. I'm so proud of you and am so excited to see the doors God is opening for you to minister to hurting women through *Beauty by God.*

To Suzie Duke and Judy Carden—my forever friends.

Shantel and Josh Davis, and Caleb, Abby, Luke, Annie and Liam—you're simply the best blessings! It was a summer I'll never forget.

Dwight Bain, Shirley Kump, Carolyn Ragland, the late Barbara Johnson, and John Howard, for allowing God to use you to launch my ministry in the nineties.

My terrific pastors: David and Caron Loveless and family—it all started with the seeds you planted in my life in 1986. Thanks for richly depositing a deep love for God and others in my life during the past decades. Know that my ministry is an extension of you and all of my dear friends at Discovery Church. I'm forever grateful to you. GO, COWBOYS!

My agent, Stephen Blount (The Quadrivium Group) and his wife, Susan—you have been a God-send. Thanks for representing me and brainstorming with me!

Jeff Carrine, Kirk and Bobbi Bane, Jeanenne Hilliard, Marshele Carter Waddell, Roger Austin, Lynda and Don Wigren, Robin Stanley, Janis Whipple, Billie Wilson, Carole Lewis, Linda Evans Shepherd and AWSA, Audrey Hector, Audrey Roberson, John and Kathy Morgan, John and Olivia Stemberger, Juda Attkisson, Adam McManus, Jeff Herring and Chance Winberry.

To Regal Books: President Bill Greig, Steve Lawson, Mark Weising and Bruce Barbour—thanks for believing in me and challenging me to write again.

Kim Bangs, thanks for all of your extra work on my contract.

To Tex and Mom: Thanks for welcoming me into your family.

To Travis, Austin and Logan: Thanks for your patience under my deadlines, and know how much I love your dad and want to cheer each of you on through life.

To my husband, Rick Rupard—next to the gift of Jesus, you are definitely my best Christmas present EVER! Thanks for proposing to me December 19, 2007, and marrying me on July 4, 2008. And thanks for loving me and encouraging me through the deadlines for this book. I love you forever!

And last, but most important—to my God. Thanks for the gift of Jesus. Without Him, I wouldn't have my greatest joy of a personal relationship with You! Thanks for Your love, Your Word and Your promises, which make this book possible.

Behind the Scenes of Encouragement Company

In 1986, as a sophomore at Stetson University, LeAnn took up Pastor David Loveless's challenge to reexamine the Bible as God's love letter and daily instructional.

Her pastor encouraged, "Even if you start reading for only five minutes a day, don't just read the Bible as boring history or irrelevant Sunday School lessons. As you read, ask the Holy Spirit to show you practical applications for your life and the lives of those you pray for, and start journaling what He tells you."

Sparked by this challenge, LeAnn started writing love letters to Jesus. Verses that LeAnn had read hundreds of times before now took on new meaning as the Bible became alive and relevant in her life. In 1992, reflecting back on her Love Letters to Jesus, she created her first personalized Scripture book on her computer for a friend, never dreaming where it would lead. As she started making other personalized gifts to encourage people at her church, and for other friends, word of mouth spread.

In 1994, LeAnn officially launched Encouragement Company™ encouraged by radio host Dwight Bain, and by reading Florence Littauer's book *Silver Boxes of Encouragement*. Then, in 1996, Ashley Howard received one of LeAnn's personalized books as a graduation gift from her dad's Aunt Carolyn. Later that year, Ashley's dad, John Howard (President of Howard Publishing Company), invited LeAnn to write her personalized Scriptures for the launch of the now popular Hugs™ books. Women of Faith speakers Barbara Johnson and Marilyn Meberg became mentors to LeAnn as she left her political career and started writing full-time.

Encouragement Company™ was profiled in Marilyn Meberg's bestselling book *I'd Rather Be Laughing:* "I felt a powerful jolt from these scriptures when I saw my name included within each one in bold print. It was as if a new translation of the Bible had been written especially from God to me."

LeAnn never dreamed that her personalized Scriptures would appear in over 7.5 million books, as well as calendars, mini books and greeting cards. While writing *Christmas Promises*, LeAnn married Rick Rupard, and relocated Encouragement Company from Orlando, Florida, to Aztec, New Mexico. Rick has three sons, Travis, Austin and Logan.

If you have a story of how God gave or fulfilled a promise in your life in a significant way, please contact LeAnn Weiss:

Encouragement Company
1409 W. Aztec Blvd., Box 563
Aztec, NM 87410
(407) 898-4410
ECblessing@cs.com

More Great Stories from Best-selling Author Leann Weiss

Valentine Promises
Heartfelt Reminders of True Love
Leann Weiss
ISBN 978.08307.46958
Available January 2009

Remember what it's like to love and be loved in this beautiful collection of love stories from LeAnn Weiss. From God's timeless love letter to real-life expressions of true love, readers will be inspired by these heartfelt displays of devotion. Speaking straight to a woman's heart are stories about enduring love, surprising love, a second chance at love, long-distance love and more. In Valentine Promises, discover how a marriage in tatters was mended and became a marriage helping others, how the power of love through a listening ear transformed a young man, how a pastor's Valentine roses for his wife became more meaningful than he knew. Throughout the book, readers will enjoy personalized Scriptures, which express the tenderness and tears of God's personal one-on-one love and care for them. Inspiring quotes, true stories about God fulfilling promises, and prayers will also remind readers that a personal relationship with the Creator and His Son brings His indescribable love straight into their hearts.